Staying Connected

in your marriage

Daily Reflections & Dialogue by

Al Francis Lacki

*"...you can have the marriage you really want,
it will happen because you make it so."*

Copyright© 1995, 2000 by Al Francis Lacki
ISBN: 0-9641428-7-2

Published by Uplift Enterprises
P.O. Box 1612
Troy, MI 48099-1612

Printed in the United States of America
10 9 8 7 6 5 4 3

Library of Congress Catalog Card Number: 99-72918

Second Edition-Revised

Book design by Larry Orlando

uplift
Enterprises

If you are unable to obtain this book from your local book seller, you
may order it directly from the publisher. Please send check or money
order in the amount of $14.00 + $2.50 for shipping and handling to:
Uplift Enterprises, P.O. Box 1612, Troy MI, 48099-1612.

E-Mail: uplift@ameritech.net
Or call: (248) 362-3340

To Julie, my wife, for her patience, loving

support and encouragement along the way.

To Michelle and Mark, for all the pleasure,

joy and love they so generously share.

Introduction

This is a book for daily personal reflection, with questions that invite you to share in dialogue with your partner. I invite you to set time aside each day to reflect on a given subject and be with your own thoughts and feelings. Then, take time each day to share with your partner. Decide who will go first. One speaks and the other listens to *understand* and *reflect back* what was said. Take turns. The questions at the end of each reflection can help you get started.

Any questions or comments you have for your partner, while in dialogue, should be mainly to obtain clarification and accuracy of understanding. The listening partner simply reflects back, without comment, interpretation or discussion. The objective is to listen and reflect back the meaning of what your partner is saying and feeling, as accurately as possible. The process may be repeated until accuracy of understanding is achieved. The message received needs to be the message heard. Further discussion and clarification is often helpful and encouraged.

The benefits from daily reflections and dialogue are: you feel good about yourself, you spend time with yourself on a regular basis, you honor your own thoughts and feelings, you learn about yourself, you learn to focus your attention, you experience quiet time, you relax, you learn patience, you feel validated, you sharpen your talking skills, you sharpen your listening skills, you experience acceptance and respect, you feel understood, you feel loved, you love more deeply, you feel more connected, you experience effective communication.

It is my hope that you commit to growing personally and together and that you renew this commitment as often as possible. The process I encourage you to use in this book can make a difference in the way you relate to each other. This is a way you can express your seriousness to remain alive and connected in your marriage.

Al Francis Lacki

Getting A Clear Direction

Although goal setting is discussed often, it is seldom done. Many of us respond to the situation at hand and have no clear direction for our lives. Setting goals helps us to define our directions more clearly. We lessen the risk of living our lives based on our whims or sudden impulses.

It can be helpful to list various areas of our life such as health, finances, career, work, spiritual life, or marriage, to name just a few, and form goals in these areas.

We may experience disappointment when we sense an absence of accomplishment in our lives. Look to your goals. Do you have any real goals that you value and persistently follow? Are your directions vague and undefined?

We can use our goals as personal standards for ourselves and thus avoid comparisons with others. We need not become discouraged if we fail or grow weary along the way—this is another year, another day to set our sights and allow ourselves to dream.

• What goals do you currently value in your marriage?
• How could clear goals and directions help you in your life and in your relationship?

Growth takes place one day at a time.

We Affect Each Other

In our marriage, we walk in and out of each other's space. This time it may be we want just a moment to chat, next time it may be longer and for a different reason. It is these comings and goings that we need to investigate. How do we make each other's day?

You can make your partner's day sometimes by walking into the room and sometimes by leaving the room. Consider what you may be bringing in and what you may be leaving behind.

Are you leaving behind an unresolved argument, a hurting partner, a cheerful smile, a silent peacefulness, a bitterness, a broken promise, a satisfied friend, an atmosphere of love and harmony? Are you bringing in a calm request, an urgent plea, a single question, a desire to be present, a special hug, a loud demand, an angry look, a condemning voice, an honest compliment?

- *What are you bringing and leaving with each other?*
- *How do you help make each other's day?*

Growth takes place one day at a time.

Checking Our Losses

At the beginning of a new year it is common to look ahead and look behind. We recognize events and people that have impacted our lives over the past year. We may even anticipate certain events and happenings down the road.

On reflection, we may encounter certain losses. These come to mind easily and cause us to have specific feelings. It is important to identify and focus on our losses. These are the most evident and the ones we notice at first glance: the loss through death, or divorce, the loss of a friendship.

The secondary losses are also vital to identify. These are often overlooked and yet are most influential. These are the side effects, additional losses we experience. We consider in more detail what our focused loss entails.

- *What losses can you and your partner identify?*
- *How have these losses impacted your relationship?*

Growth takes place one day at a time.

Come To Our Senses

Isn't it "lovely," "darling," "good," "nice," "awesome"? These are just some of the ways we use to simplify things into one word. The fact is, however, that sometimes we experience an inadequacy to say more or even explain just what it is we take in with our senses. We take in the information we stockpile for ourselves with our senses. It is these senses that we need to come to for help when we experience life as boring and stale. These are our roads to awareness and aliveness.

When we take responsibility for what we see, hear, taste, touch, and smell, we open ourselves to our personal experiences and we can share those with each other.

We speak for no one but ourselves. It is in so doing that we encourage self expression from each other and identify these daily experiences as rich exchanges in our marriage.

Are you coming to your senses? They are special.

- *Which of your senses are you most aware of?*
- *How do you strive to keep your senses alive and vibrant?*
- *How could the sharpening of your senses improve the quality of your life and your relationship?*

Growth takes place one day at a time.

Share In Others' Hopes

From different sources around us, we are being asked to contribute to the hope of others. It may come in the form of a request from our church or congregation. It may come from a charitable cause or organization.

Our sense of compassion may or may not cause us to respond. It may be that we simply respond out of an awareness of our own abundance. We may recognize the needs around us in a less dramatic way. We may even experience a sense of helplessness in the light of such heavy demands and be tempted to reduce our compassion by responding that "it is just too much for one person to respond." The shift to making it the responsibility of "bigger people" than us, or "let the government or church supply" is a tempting one indeed. Instead, we should try not to undermine our personal compassion and look for smaller ways to share our resources and give others hope.

Are there such individuals and opportunities around us? Take another look and discuss the possibilities.

> • *What resources do you have that could possibly*
> *bring solace and comfort to others?*
> • *How could you best share from your resources?*

Growth takes place one day at a time.

Living With Uncertainties

We acknowledge, perhaps with some difficulty, that it is not easy to live with uncertainty in our lives. This acknowledgement, however, seems vital in opening us to a greater trust and cooperation. We can begin to trust our own experiences and recognize these experiences as honest and trustworthy.

This may be very rewarding for us and contribute to a greater sense of optimism about our life. It encourages hope and nourishes healthy and vibrant relationships with other people in our lives.

Can you truly trust in your uncertainty, and in your ability to recognize an opportunity that can promote greater happiness and peace for you? What role does the uncertainty in your life play?

• What are the areas of uncertainty in your life?
• How do these uncertainties affect your personal life?
Your marriage?

Growth takes place one day at a time.

Our Belief About Others

The way we take in the people around us can have a strong impact on us. We need to be aware of our beliefs about the people nearest to us. This allows us to consider how important it is to trust our beliefs.

We can learn to become more patient and tolerant when they disagree or do things differently than us. Our experiences with those close to us reminds us more of human error and frailty than any evil intention or meanness. We can be more open and accepting of them without seeing their behavior as evidence of not loving us or having malicious intent.

This does not necessarily mean we agree with everything they do or say. When we attribute to others evil or malicious intent we run the risk of distancing ourselves from them.

Discuss your beliefs and attitudes with each other regarding this matter.

> • *How do these beliefs affect you and your*
> *relationship with each other?*
> • *Do you believe in a basic goodness in people?*

Growth takes place one day at a time.

Now Is The Time

I have noticed the words "Just do it" on T-shirts. It is a forthright and direct statement that reminds me of how important it is to cut through some things and "simply just do it." Often, we get hung up on our interpretation of the situation in terms of our own fears and unrealistic expectations.

I was thinking of Jesus' statement to his followers when he saw the large crowd before him and his devoted followers were in the mood for discussing how they were going to feed all those people. Jesus told them directly, "You do it." We hear a lot today about the poor and needy in our towns and cities. We can discuss it, put it up to a vote and simply argue the case. We can also cut through it all and find our own personal response to the situation and "just do it."

When we are hungry or thirsty and in need of food we usually do not debate the issue very long or send it to committee, do we? Was Jesus naive?

• Are there any situations, problems, decisions, or opportunities
that need an immediate response in your life?
• How could such a response add to the
quality of your relationship?

Growth takes place one day at a time.

Allowing Others In

Just as we need to monitor what comes into our minds, we need to monitor people who come into our lives, especially relatives and friends who mean well and have only our welfare in mind. Even our well-intentioned children can demand, force and expect in innocent ways. We need to draw boundaries for others and identify those times that are ours. It is amazing how many parents don't have locks an their bedroom doors.

Sometimes outside influences are more important to you than your partner. After all, it's your family, your boss, or your friend. It may not matter that it is dinner time or an already planned weekend. Draw attention to the importance of your time together and work toward an understanding and solution to your situation. It may be an answering service that is needed, a babysitter even when you are at home, a marked calender that notifies you of your priority to be alone with each other. You have the ability to define needs and wants while protecting your relationship from unsolicited outside company.

• How protective are you of your time together?
• How can you together monitor the outside influences on your relationship?
• What can you do alone and together to provide for Quantity and Quality time?

Growth takes place one day at a time.

Share The Responsibility

When we struggle with problems in our relationships, we often have great difficulty identifying the problem. Sometimes we experience frustration and confusion in our efforts to find the causes for our pain and discomfort.

We are tempted to seek vague solutions and even mystical reasons to serve as explanations. We may tend to blame others or something outside of ourselves so as not to face our own possible contribution to the problem.

We must be careful not to promote deception by offering excuses and allowing our protective devices to cut off those more open and honest contributions for which we are ultimately responsible.

Let us help by asking each other for support and encouragement in our efforts to first identify our problems. Then ask how we might be contributing to their existence and keeping them afloat.

> • *What problems can you identify in your relationship*
> *at this time?*
> • *What do each of you do to help maintain these problems?*
> • *What can each of you do that would*
> *contribute to solving them?*

Growth takes place one day at a time.

Going Beyond Ourselves

Consider the possible reasons and the motivations behind what you do. It could be your generosity, your sense of fairness, your caring and willingness to support each other and others in the family. These and other reasons can be the hidden motivations that give meaning to our existence, to our commitments and to the success we make of our lives.

Though we continue to make each other and our families the primary receivers of our concern and caring, we know we must go beyond and reach outside these natural circles of people. It is vital for us to direct some of our energy and interest outside and when we do, we seem to energize our own inner circle of family and friends in a new way.

We may find ourselves involved in a new interest, or an old interest or project or religious experience that resurfaces and takes on new meaning. This may be one person or even both of you getting involved and going beyond yourselves as a couple, as a family.

- *What gets you excited and involved with others?*
- *How do you share your excitement and interests with your partner?*

Growth takes place one day at a time.

A Marriage View

Our words can reflect our views and attitudes about marriage. The words "I got married" reflect a passive view of marriage. It is a view that is understandable, however, considering that in many instances we have all been presented marriage as a static and passive institution. It is referred to as a state of life in which we have something "done to us." Such a view may prompt us to wait around for someone or something to direct us and move us along.

Can you afford to maintain this passive view and the retiring attitudes without risking stagnation and boredom?

- *Can you identify with this view of marriage?*
- *What impact could such a view have in terms of the effort you are making to grow as a couple?*

Growth takes place one day at a time.

Marriage Power

We often think of power as a strength and specifically in terms of might, force, and coercion. We can certainly identify it with the military and even associate it to politics and those who have it over others in one way or another.

A more positive way of viewing power is to understand it as anything that enables us to fulfill our purpose, whatever that may be.

In a marriage, each needs to know he or she is being taken seriously. This is a form of power. When we feel we are not taken seriously, listened to with respect for what we say, we can easily determine that what we say, feel or do makes no difference. We then can experience a sense of frustration and a deeper sense of powerlessness. Real power involves shared strength and rules out the need for any control or domination.

• Do you experience power in your relationship as a positive and necessary ingredient for the success of your marriage?
• How could you nurture this power in each other?

Growth takes place one day at a time.

Don't Put Me Off

"Hold on," "I'll be right there," "It will take just a minute." How often have we heard these or others like them from our children, partner, or others? These are statements that can aggravate us, test our patience, and cause us frustration and anger.

Yet, when we think about it, perhaps we have put our own selves off at times. We have an inspiration, a noble thought, that could blossom into some productive activity and maybe we tell ourselves, "hold on," "not too fast," "maybe later." This of course does not suggest that we be imprudent and rush right off into something impulsively. It does suggest, however, that we recognize those surprise moments in our lives that beckon us to respond when we experience a call to perform some service that could benefit another, or even ourselves.

- *What action, product or decision have you
or your partner been putting off?*
- *How could you treat those sudden inspirations, inner calls
and quiet whispers in your life with respect and care?*

Growth takes place one day at a time.

Peace In Our World

For some of us there is general concern for the safety of our world. There are global unrest and feelings of fear and anxiety. Those who have come for their counseling session with me have expressed these worries, fears, and confusion. Some of us seek guidance in God and are petitioning earnestly that we have peace. At times of general unrest, our own personal problems seem so insignificant and we move out of ourselves and into a larger vision of our world. We experience the world shrinking before our very eyes and names of places that once were just names suddenly become household words echoing strong feelings and serious pleas for peace. Please God, let there be peace on earth and in our hearts today.

> • *Are you at peace within yourself and with each other*
> *at this moment in time?*
> • *What could you do to promote and maintain peace*
> *in your life, your marriage, your home, your work?*

Growth takes place one day at a time.

Sharing Our Power

Ideally, as husband and wife, we should have the same degree of power in our marriage relationship. Hopefully, there is no top dog and under dog relationship. This ideal, however, is seldom achieved and we acknowledge that despite good intentions we enter into control maneuvers with each other. We try to reduce these maneuvers whenever we can by substituting respect, the ability to negotiate our differences and nourish our daily intentions to share openly and honestly.

Our intimacy depends upon this shared power. We can then be open, vulnerable, and share our innermost thoughts and feelings without fear of reprisals or discounts. Without equality and risk-taking, honest communication is not likely to occur. A way of monitoring your equality is to consider your cooperation with each other and your ability to work and live together as a team.

• How much of a role does control play in your marriage?
•What can you do personally and together to promote respect, acceptance, and goodwill in your relationship?

Growth takes place one day at a time.

Clarify Your Boundaries

Boundaries or limits are acknowledged necessities in our efforts to maintain well-functioning relationships. It is necessary to be able to tell what is mine and what is yours. What are my intentions and feelings and what are yours?

These, however, are not rigid to the extent that we cannot maintain a certain flow, a give and take. Sometimes our boundaries are stretched or we stretch them ourselves in the midst of arguments or passion. It is not that another takes us over but it is a kind of inability at the time to define clearly our feelings, thoughts, and intentions.

The fortunate thing, however, is that we can regroup and set our boundaries in place after a certain time has lapsed. When our feelings come out, we let go and our past can often get mixed with our present. Not a great deal makes sense at the time. The question is, can we come back later to look for solutions and experience ourselves intact.

- *On what issues in your marriage have you taken a definite stand ?*
- *What steps are you willing to take that would help define and clarify the boundaries you want to maintain in your relationship?*
- *How can you help each other in this matter?*

Growth takes place one day at a time.

Learning From Our Past

When we are troubled in our marriage there often appears the question, "where is this coming from?" The current situation we find ourselves in seems to lack an explanation or an answer.

Our growing up experiences have had a powerful impact on us in terms of our attitudes, beliefs, feelings, and expectations. We can experience ourselves reacting and acting now in ways we may have experienced at some time in our past.

The important thing is to recognize and identify these past influences and use them as guides to assist us in living our lives in the present. They need not bind or restrict us from living our lives with purpose and direction.

Can you assess your current feelings, thoughts, and behavior and experiment with options other than what you currently experience? Your ability to appreciate and use your creativity can benefit you personally and as a couple.

- *What positive influences did you bring to your marriage?*
- *What negative influences did you bring to your marriage?*
- *What characteristic do you have that you wish
your partner had ? Why?*

Growth takes place one day at a time.

Autonomy - Winning Ways

Ideally, we want to be true to ourselves, know what we think, feel and do, take full responsibility for all of this and make the choices we believe we need to make. This is the definition of autonomy put simply.

Perhaps we sense the importance of being autonomous because we can tie it in to our own sense of who we are. We come to know how all of this fits together when we consider how we respect each other's thoughts, feelings, and actions.

Do we really experience freedom to say and feel and do what we think, believe, and feel? This goes a long way in assisting us with making the choices we need to make in the circumstances we are in. We need not be in competition with each other. We can negotiate our differences and come up as winners instead of losers.

*• How do you encourage and feel encouraged
to make your thoughts, feelings, and needs known?
• How do you respectfully deal with your differences?*

Growth takes place one day at a time.

The Art Of Listening

The flip side of talking is listening. As a couple, both must be actively involved in the communication process. Listening is a very powerful art in its own right. It is a difficult but rewarding art.

One of the ways we can know if we are listening is to know if the other person argues or disagrees with our understanding of what they are saying. Is it more common to tell another what they said than asking them? We can check out with each other what it is we thought we heard. This would be very helpful and it would tell us that we are on the right track. To have someone in our life that truly listens to us is a blessing indeed. How important is listening to you?

•Can you recall experiencing yourself being truly listened to? How did you feel?
•What was present or occurring that let you know that you were truly being listened to?

Growth takes place one day at a time.

The Eyes Really Say It

Some professional football players are wearing tinted plastic to cover their eyes so as not to give the opposition the opportunity to "read" their eyes. Our eyes carry much of what we think, feel, and intend to do. People can "see" us through our eyes.

What do you say with your eyes? What do you look or watch for? Become aware of what you fix your gaze upon. Are you aware of the power in your gaze? Do they set off a little twinkle so as to tell another when you have completed your communication? Do you lower them in shyness or lack of confidence? Do you use them to push someone away when you are angry? Is your gaze locked in on what is good and beautiful? Is that same gaze even locked in to what is wrong with others? Do you see more of what is wrong and does it ever seem like there is a disproportionate attention focused on faults and mistakes? These could provide you with a personal challenge to consider the power in your eyes.

- *Share your thoughts and feelings regarding the questions above.*

Growth takes place one day at a time.

Be Merciful

One of the beatitudes or be-happy attitudes is to be merciful. If we are, then we can expect God will treat us in like manner.

Perhaps we can more easily understand being merciful to another when we picture someone like Mother Theresa on the streets of Calcutta. To experience mercy from another or to be merciful to another may seem foreign to us at first. We may consider it in a setting or position that is connected with justice.

Longfellow says, "Mercy becomes more a magistrate than the vindictive wrath which men call justice." Cervantes states "Among the attributes of God, although they are all equal, mercy shines even more brilliantly than justice."

Mercy does not judge–it loves. It forgives. It does not see weakness. It sees need and it reaches out to touch.

- *Have you ever been touched by mercy?*
- *Can you relive the moment?*
- *Can you see yourself called to be merciful to another?*

Growth takes place one day at a time.

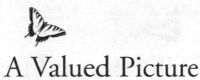

A Valued Picture

The experts, whether secular or religious, remind us that our health originates in our self-image and self-esteem. The picture we have of ourselves changes with the passing of years and circumstances in our lives. This comprises our self-image. The value we place on each of these pictures as we experience them gives us our self-esteem.

How do we judge ourselves? Again, this will vary, as one day we value ourselves as successful and another day unsuccessful. Over the years we develop a certain consistency and we are fortunate if that consistency favors a more positive value of ourselves. It can tell us how things are going in our life at a particular time.

> • *What is the picture you have most consistently of yourself?*
> • *How is your self-esteem?*
> • *Are you valuing yourself?*
> • *Are you experiencing yourself valued by others,*
> *especially your partner?*

Growth takes place one day at a time.

An Honest Appraisal

When we value and appreciate ourselves, we feel good about ourselves and the world around us. We generally are optimistic and self-assured.

It is important that we know how to deal with our own imperfections. We need to see ourselves realistically and in the light of our humanness. Sometimes this is difficult and we can experience ourselves competing with others. We need to be our own best booster and cheer ourselves on in our journey in life. We can hold firm and not allow ourselves to become discouraged.

Someone once said, "A hypocrite is not someone who fails to live up to their standard–that's a human being, a hypocrite is dishonest." Honesty with ourselves is often difficult, challenging and very rewarding. This can be an important goal for us–to attempt to see and value ourselves as we truly are. What a marvelous goal to pursue and share.

- *What do you do alone and together to encourage and foster honesty and openness in your relationship?*
- *How can you become your own best booster and cheer yourself and your partner on in your marriage journey?*

Growth takes place one day at a time.

Responding To The Challenge

It is difficult not to compare ourselves with others, especially at times when we experience ourselves on the losing end. We often sharpen our vision to spot all the advantages on the other side and stress the disadvantages that are on our side.

At times, someone comes along who we see battered by unfortunate happenings and we wonder how they remain standing. We may even notice another who is not coping very well.

What do you notice about yourself? Do you experience yourself struggling to respond to the different obstacles and challenges in your own life? In your own marriage?

How are you coping? What is the source of your strength? Is there some way today that you can connect with your own struggles and evaluate your coping strengths and weaknesses? Consider some of your most valuable resources. God, your partner, your family, your friends, the power within you.

- *What coping strategies do you and your partner use to deal with the various challenges you face in your marriage?*
- *Are they successful? If not, why not?*
- *What resources are available to you at this time?*

Growth takes place one day at a time.

Loving And Doing

Valuing ourselves and maintaining a healthy, positive self-image and self-esteem are some of the most important gifts we can give to ourselves. We run the risk, however, of trying to make it all happen by simply doing a lot of things.

Society praises achievement and well it should, but it can also cloud our vision and invite us to consider our achievements as the only means for holding ourselves in esteem. Thus, when we are not achieving, we can then conclude that we are not of value. We run the risk of driving ourselves and preoccupying ourselves with a process that can lead to workaholism.

We should love ourselves because we are lovable as we are. We can bring joy and satisfaction to our work. Our work then becomes the valued experience because we are already good and lovable and this enhances what we do.

- *Is your love conditioned by what you do*
  and what is done for you? How so?
- *How does the current climate in your relationship affect*
  the way you feel about yourself and each other?

Growth takes place one day at a time.

Have A Balanced Time

Some of us spend much of our thought in the past-mistakes we have made, should haves that never occurred, and painful past events. Some of us, on the other hand, deny our past or attempt to block it out of our memories and thus never learn anything from our history.

Then there are some of us who live only in the present. We go for the gusto and live for the day. But we need to also consider our future and have a glimpse of what lies ahead.

All in all, we need to have a balance. Living fully alive in the present, with a respect and openness to learning from our past, and a realistic expectation and vision of what could be ahead. It is when we exaggerate one of these time areas that we run into difficulty. What is your current experience?

- *Do you have a balance involving past, present, and future?*
- *How does your orientation help or not help your marriage?*
- *What impact does your personal balance, or lack of it, have upon your relationship?*

Growth takes place one day at a time.

An Invitation To Grow

Attempting to become all that we can be is difficult to envision and understand. This is true for us as individuals and as couples. The process involved can be unclear and somewhat mysterious. We are asked to stretch our imagination. It is leaving behind some of our old ways of seeing and doing things. It is risky.

Growing beckons us to direct our lives. We are often challenged to break from the past in certain ways and shed certain childhood needs and dependencies. This can be painful, not only for ourselves, but for those we love and live with. Growing as a couple is challenging. It involves an openness to learning and changing as a couple. Old ideals, promises, and behaviors need to be evaluated in the light of where we are now and what we want to become as a couple.

- *What does growing as a couple mean to you?*
- *Is it a meaning you share easily with each other?*
- *How could this become a goal for your marriage?*

Growth takes place one day at a time.

You Are Personally Responsible

I am the only one in the best position to discover who I am. You are the best for you. This does not mean we always act on that belief. We often want to transfer responsibility for who we are onto someone else. Of course, there will always be someone around who is more than willing to accommodate us.

Discovering myself, however, is a personal task. It means I take responsibility for my thoughts, my feelings, my intentions, as well as my actions. I take it upon myself to define myself.

It is important to consider how others evaluate me and what my partner thinks of what I say and do, but it is of equal importance that I have a personal assessment ready. This short circuits the chance that I will use my partner's evaluation as a guide over my own. Our own, of course, should never be cast in stone.

In our marriage we want to consider how each may be forfeiting personal responsibility.

• How personally responsible do you hold yourself for your happiness, the direction of your life, and the direction of your marriage?
• How do you help foster and encourage personal responsibility with each other?

Growth takes place one day at a time.

It Is Never Too Late To Learn

Some of us do not "come to" until late in life. We seem to awaken somehow and it can be a happy or sad experience.

Often, it is both a sudden realization that we neglected this or that and a more mellow composure to simply accept and look for the good. This often happens when we turn our attention to those "things" we always considered vital and essential.

Love may have been set aside or compromised in favor of economic gain or the pursuit of some self-interest. Without a lot of practice, we may believe we don't know how to tell another we love them. We even revert back to such an oldie as "you should know how much I love you by now."

Love needs to be shown and it needs to be said.

*• Does your relationship provide an atmosphere and
an encouragement for you to learn, develop, and grow?
If so, how? If not, why not?
• How could learning become a great antidote
to boredom in your marriage?*

Growth takes place one day at a time.

Loving Is Learned

Our families provided us with our first school for learning. Some of us learned enough and some of us didn't.

Loving is first a family affair. If it was expressed openly and consistently, chances are we feel good about ourselves and others. Some of us did not get enough. We were the oldest, responsible for taking care of somebody else. Somehow it never came around to our turn. We may have been the youngest and maybe we received it all. We may be the middle child and the peacemaker in the family. We had to be different from the one above and the one below. After all, we had to have our special place too.

How can this all have meaning for our marriage? Well, it can help if we attempt to understand and appreciate where we came from and the birth order we experienced.

• How was love expressed and received when you were growing up?
• How is love expressed and experienced now
in your marriage relationship?

Growth takes place one day at a time.

Believe In Each Other

One of the tasks of a good therapist is to support the client's efforts at trying to become the person he or she truly wants to be. This comes in the form of understanding and encouragement. Ideally, we want to support each other in our marriage. We need to recognize that like ourselves, our partner can change, grow, and continue to unfold. Otherwise, we see our partner remaining stagnant and our vision is limited for ourselves and each other.

Believing in our partner involves active support. It needs to include going out of our way to provide practical help so that he or she can dream dreams and reach goals, strengthen his or her life and stretch emotionally, intellectually, and spiritually. This strengthens our faith and confidence in each other. We need to encourage each other to become the best we can be. Are you attempting to do this with each other?

• How are you encouraging each other to grow personally in your marriage?
•What are the ways you are supporting each other currently in your relationship?

Growth takes place one day at a time.

Respect Is The Bottom Line

Some marriages do not survive the test of time because one or both partners become disappointed and disillusioned. We can blind ourselves not only to the good in each other but also to the other's faults and unattractiveness.

A way of contributing to the success and growth in our marriage is to continue doing for each other the things we once did, especially the things that make us proud and pleased to be with each other. The bottom line for all of this is the promotion of respect, a very powerful force in everyone's life. It shows up in those little ways we say "thank you," "please," and "I am sorry." This helps avoid taking each other for granted.

Of course, there are the unattractive, hurtful things we experience. Nobody is perfect. We all have our weaknesses. This is a part of who we are. We do not want to only see the good. We want to admit that there are weaknesses in every marriage, including our own.

- *Is respect an active ingredient in your relationship?*
- *How do you show respect to each other?*
- *Why is it considered to be the forgotten attribute in marriage?*

Growth takes place one day at a time.

Those Unexpected Changes

There are many stories of what happens after the marriage ceremony. Some are not so funny. Often, they are stories about the changes in the lives of the couple. These include the anticipated changes after the marriage. We are often not ready for what we experience. We marry believing that given some time and combinations of goodwill and talent, we can change the other person...no such luck.

In fact, this approach has led to drastic results and often the failure of the relationship. It is difficult for some of us to believe that marrying is not a solution to our problems. Supporting each other and avoiding criticism and demands will strengthen our relationship. Accepting outbursts and tantrums from our partner is not an easy task. That is understandable. Wanting our partner to shape up immediately is also unrealistic. We may not know how to shape up our behaviors. We cannot force change. Understanding and support are crucial.

- *What changes have you experienced in your relationship since marriage?*
- *How have you and your partner tried to deal with these changes?*

Growth takes place one day at a time.

Keeping Our Promises

One of the ways we help build trust and confidence with each other is by doing what we say we are going to do. Telling our partner, especially with a sober face that, "Promises are meant to be broken" is not going to build trust. Keeping our end of the bargain, especially one that is entered jointly, needs to be honored. When, for some reason, we cannot honor a commitment, it is best to come right out and say it. "I will not clean the bathroom today." This need not be taken as a cop out.

It is important that we follow through with our promises to each other. We need to keep our word. Our word needs to mean something. This goes a long way in building the needed trust in each other. It also adds to the flavor of an ongoing cooperation. We feel good personally and we feel good about each other.

• Is your word believable? We build our trust daily this way.
• Is your partner's word believable?
*• How does keeping your word help build trust
and confidence in each other?*

Growth takes place one day at a time.

February 5

Support Each Other's Successes

One of the significant aspects of growing as a couple is one that is easily overlooked. It is the recognition and the support of our partners when they make any kind of personal, positive change in their life. It may be a job advancement, it may be an effort finally made, a decision to get rid of an old habit, or simply the reading of a book or the writing of a letter.

We can tell our partners what we notice and that we want to be a part of their growth in life. We can find ways to celebrate their successes. It need not be lavish but it certainly can be meaningful: a special meal, a card, flowers, or a family gathering. We can draw attention to such changes in sensitive and meaningful ways. We might also want to check with our partners whether they can and will go along with the celebration. Some of us are a bit guarded about such things. You can bet your efforts will be appreciated.

- *How are successes, large and small, acknowledged, supported, and celebrated in your relationship?*
- *Do you and your partner view your marriage as a growing place to be? If so, how? If not, why not?*

Growth takes place one day at a time.

Revealing Where We Stand

When we encounter each other in hurtful and discounting ways, it is rather easy to blame and justify our anger in retaliation. It can be more productive if, at those times, we find a way to define our boundaries and take responsibility for what is going on inside us. By saying, "When you speak to me in that tone of voice, I feel angry and I want to storm out of the room...I don't want to leave the scene under these circumstances...but I will not respond to you when you raise your voice at me," we set our boundaries and we avoid blaming or threatening.

It is important to understand how we need to practice a straight way of telling our partners where we stand. We need to know each other's limits. Spelling out clearly when we feel personally threatened or when our relationship is in danger of becoming undermined, can be sufficient cause for toughening up our love for each other. Toughness is not aggression. It is telling each other where we stand.

• *How do you make your position on matters of importance to you, known to your partner?*
• *How can you avoid mind reading and support and encourage self-disclosure with each other?*

Growth takes place one day at a time.

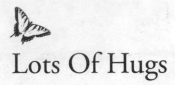

Lots Of Hugs

There are numerous references in the growth literature to the healthy benefits of hugging. Some of us can do it easily while others are more inhibited and reserved. It is important to be relaxed and genuine. Hugs, like kisses can lose their meaning when given in a matter-of-fact way or as simple ritual. Can you imagine a television commercial prescribing three hugs a day instead of three tablets of such and such? Give hugs a try if you do not include these in your relationship each day. They work. Oh yes, if you are mostly the giver of the hugs, experience yourself receiving. If you are mostly the receiver, experience yourself giving. Have fun noticing each other and feeling the warm fuzzies.

> • *How do you give hugs to each other?*
> • *How do you receive hugs from each other?*

Growth takes place one day at a time.

Time To Say Thanks

There are many people who enter and exit our lives daily. Each one brings their uniqueness and specialness to us. These may be parents, spouse, children, friend, clergymen, co-worker, and others that we come in contact with. In a very real sense we are affected, though we may not always know how.

Perhaps you can think of a couple that has influenced you in some positive way. What was it about them or what did they do that impressed or influenced you? Maybe it was one person who contributed something in a certain way to your personal and marriage growth. This is a good time to recognize that person or that couple and what their influence has meant to you. You may wish to express your appreciation to them directly. A phone call or card may be just the thing. It could brighten up their lives, as well as yours.

- *Share with your partner your thoughts, feelings, and the possible actions you could take involving the above material.*

Growth takes place one day at a time.

What We Say About Ourselves

Often we have the best of intentions. We mean well and present ourselves to others the best we can. Do you realize that your communication with others contains the basic message of how you really feel about yourself? Consider how you feel in the presence of others. Do you feel relaxed, self-confident and composed? Are you your own best booster?

Listen to any self-messages that would denigrate or be interpreted as self-discounting. Messages that go on internally in all of us are not always easily accessible unless we become more tuned into ourselves. Pay attention to your experiences first with the people close to you–those you live with, your spouse and children. Listen to your conversation with them and experience your thoughts and feelings. Proceed on to your experience with your friends and those you work with.

- *How are you feeling about yourself*
when you are with your partner?
- *What message about yourself do you think*
you send to others?

Growth takes place one day at a time.

We All Have Touchy Spots

The story is told of a young man who was very self-conscious of his looks and his one eye in particular. It remained stationary due to a biological complication in the eye itself. He eventually gained a reputation for being shy and aloof. He was even referred to by his friends as "wood eye." One day, after many attempts to overcome his shyness, he noticed a girl at work who seemed to be shy and aloof. He decided that day to approach her and ask her for a date. After a brief introduction he asked, "Would you care to go out with me?" She responded quickly, "Would I, would I!" He immediately responded with, "Big nose, big nose!"

Our perception and how we accept ourselves is often reflected in the way we respond to others. Are you defensive and protective of yourself in ways that may suggest some touchy areas that need your further attention? We all have some. It helps to share them. Discovery can be fun.

- *What are the things your partner says or does that cause a defensive reaction in you?*
- *What do you say or do that causes a defensive reaction in your partner?*

Growth takes place one day at a time.

Taking A Breather

For a variety of reasons, we may feel discouraged to the point of questioning the value of what we are doing. In some ways we wonder about the sense of it all. If so, we could be at the threshold of breaking through some self-protective walls and into a process of self-discovery that could be very valuable and enriching.

We sometimes give ourselves a report card that lines up all the mistakes and failures with few, if any, pluses. This is probably one-sided and may reflect the need for more accurate assessment of what is going on in our life.

Personal and prayerful time alone could be helpful and point to some areas that may need assessment and attention. Taking a little time out for yourself may be the order for today. Take some quiet time and take another look.

> • *What are some loose ends that leave you uncertain,*
> *confused, or worried today?*
> • *How can today's personal assessment and sharing with*
> *your partner benefit you and your relationship?*

Growth takes place one day at a time.

God Give Me The Serenity

"Beyond a wholesome discipline, be gentle with yourself. You are a child of the universe–no less than the trees and the stars. You have a right to be here. And whether or not it is clear to you, no doubt the universe is unfolding like it should." (Desiderata).

The universe is perfect. It is exactly as it should be. Yet, we often have plans of our own and make demands that the world "should" be something different. This leads us to the next step which seems so short a distance away and is contained in the expression, "if only." Neither helps attain peace of mind or the truth. We can distort our view of the world with unfounded demands and complaints of unfairness. This can lead to bemoaning our plight and living in a cruel world.

Another way is to accept what is, change what we can, and thank God for knowing the difference. The latter is accurate and expresses much wisdom.

•In what areas of your relationship do you find yourself lacking?
• What areas do you need to learn to accept?
• What areas do you want to change?

Growth takes place one day at a time.

We Are Special, And That's That

We all require a healthy dose of self-esteem in order to feel lovable and important. This lovableness and importance is rooted in our special relationship to God.

Who we are in our own mind's eye will often set the stage for the value judgments we make about ourselves and leads to the feelings we experience. What we feel, what we do, does not make us who we are. We are much more. When we become aware and believe in our own goodness, we can avoid those destructive self messages that have us discounting ourselves and others.

Being our own best friend, our own cheerleader, is not being selfish nor egotistical. We are simply recognizing the truth of who and what we are. This can then allow us to open ourselves up to the world around us, and permit ourselves to enter into honest and meaningful relationships. Our goodness need never be on trial. We may second guess and question everything else.

- *Why is it so important for you to own your own specialness?*
- *How does your partner add or detract from that specialness?*

Growth takes place one day at a time.

48

A Bridge To Your Partner

If having a positive self-image and self-esteem is so vital to our spiritual and emotional welfare, it would seem to follow that we would want this not only for ourselves, but for everyone else and especially our partner. This can truly be the goal of every marriage. We know that self-esteem cannot be injected or sprayed on. Would that it could be so. It can only come from within ourselves.

We can, however, set the climate in which this self-esteem can flourish. We can build a bridge to our partners through the powerful process of caring and loving listening. We can help enable our partners to appreciate and experience themselves in ways that promote a value of self.

Consider the place and value of listening in your personal life and in your marriage. The richness and power of loving listening is one of the best kept secrets in our world.

> • *How well do you listen to each other?*
> • *What are you willing to do personally and together*
> *to improve your listening skills?*

Growth takes place one day at a time.

The Gifts In Each Other

"The greatest gift to another is not to reveal our riches to them, but rather, to reveal theirs to themselves." These are the words of the late Cardinal Suenens, Archbishop of Belgium.

In order to be caring and loving partners we must learn to appreciate the gifts existing in each other. One of those gifts is our specialness and the specialness of our partner. God made him or her special and we know He does not make junk. This truth colors and gives meaning as we make an effort to see and experience that other magnificent person, our partner, in a special way. There are truths and riches in our partners.

You can come to believe in that person and what he or she says will be truthful. There is no real reason not to believe in that person, because you have already come to trust what they say. You don't second guess each other. Your partner can begin to believe in the power of their own goodness. We begin to experience ourselves appreciated and taken seriously. This is the meaning of power in a loving relationship.

- *What are the special qualities you appreciate in each other?*
- *How are you nurturing these qualities?*
- *How do you experience these qualities with each other?*

Growth takes place one day at a time.

Listening More Deeply

Discovering the need that lies under our complaints is essential in getting at the truth while encouraging each other to grow. It is no easy task and depending on our own well-being at the time, we can experience ourselves annoyed and frustrated. It is an opportunity for greater understanding and allowing us to deal with our true needs.

When we are disappointed and hold back our comments, it may be because we want to avoid hurting the other. When we complain of having too much to do, it may be that we are expressing our desire to be close and intimate.

Can you look for the hidden positive needs that lie within some of your complaints and what they may be trying to say? It gives us another way of looking and seeing what could really be going on in our lives and with each other. This can make for an interesting and healthy relationship. It will also take time and patient effort.

> • *How do you deal with each other's complaints?*
> • *How could you help each other discover the needs and wants underlying those complaints?*

Growth takes place one day at a time.

A Cooperative Effort

At this time in our society, many husbands and wives work outside the home. For some, this is working out just fine. For others, it brings stress and tension. Often, we have to negotiate a number of options so as to maintain marriage stability.

One of the necessary questions is, "How do we share the load at home?" This can be asked by either one. It cannot become merely a question of men do this and women do that. This is often a carry-over from what our experience had been while growing up in our families and watching what mom and dad did. Some division of labor needs to be sorted out. This can be done by mutually deciding on what areas or tasks need attention. It is not a question of, "O.K., I'll help you." It needs to carry the weight of "us." We are in this together.

Take some time to sort out the needs and see who gets what to do. This is a joint effort. This could be a great beginning and well worth the effort.

- *How are you fostering cooperation in your marriage?*
- *What can each of you do to encourage and develop a more cooperative team effort?*

Growth takes place one day at a time.

Not Always A 50-50 Arrangement

Our love for each other needs to be consistent and, therefore, cannot always depend on how we feel. It needs to manifest itself through our actions. Picking up the slack when the other is unable or unwilling to carry the load is not an uncommon occurrence. Our willingness to sacrifice our own convenience and bracket our personal needs in favor of helping and reaching out to our partner can strengthen and build our marriage.

Of course, we must be careful lest we count ourselves among the many who feel manipulated and martyred. This can occur when our boundaries become blurred in our relationship, and the necessary element of reciprocity does not exist. We can feel burdened and resentful when our love and generosity has little or no return. Always "giving in" can cause us to deny ourselves and live in and through our partner. This, in the long run, is counterproductive.

Consider these aspects in light of your own marriage.

- *How do you "pick up the slack" when one does not want to or can't do their fair share?*
- *How can you prevent manipulation from occurring in your relationship?*

Growth takes place one day at a time.

Strength In Conflict

Someone once said we are like tea bags. We don't know how strong we are until we are in hot water. We all have problems. This is a given for every marriage. Yet, many of us will do anything to avoid problems. We have difficulty imagining there being any merit or value in having problems. We either become fearful or we discount our ability to resolve them.

It is only when we accept the reality of problems in our life that we can get on with the task of learning to solve them constructively, and experience the exhilaration that can come from solving or managing a problem. The strength that we can experience when we deal with our conflict and problems adds to the zest and security we so want for ourselves.

Take time with each other and consider your approach to the conflicts and problems you face and anticipate in your marriage relationship.

- *What is your approach to the conflicts in your relationship?*
- *Does the resolution of your conflicts leave you strengthened or weary?*

Growth takes place one day at a time.

Assessing Our Fears

Fear is a crippler. It can cause us to misdirect our focus in life and drain us of our creative energy. It can reduce our effectiveness as persons and bring about painful consequences in our relationships. It often involves the combination of a fight or flight response to a perceived set of circumstances in our lives. This is normal. We get into trouble when we do not recognize that these responses are not working. It is not helpful to deny or avoid the situation before us.

It can be helpful to recognize that we may be assessing ourselves as being in "over our head." We need a careful assessment of the situation and of our ability to handle it. It may be time to ask for help. It also may be time to be prepared to walk away. These alternatives are not easy to face. Yet, all of us meet fear in our lives.

Are these fears preventing you from reaching your personal goals, or the goals in your marriage? It may be time for a personal and joint assessment.

- *What are your fears?*
- *How are you dealing with them?*
- *How do these fears impact your relationship?*

Growth takes place one day at a time.

Wounded But Not Crushed

It is much easier to recall the good times than the bad times. We tend to avoid the failures, the disappointments, the frustrations, the brokenness in our lives. They are painful to recall. Yet, the healing of these experiences lies not in their avoidance but in embracing them. This is tough. We all have been broken in some way, often in unexpected ways and by unsuspecting people and institutions.

Facing tragedy and sorrow in our lives can be more than a burden. It can also be the door to greater growth and aliveness for us. We may even discover that when we feel brought to our knees with a heavy burden, either self-imposed or caused by another, we can still operate successfully from a kneeling position.

God is closer than we may think. We need His help and guidance. Why not ask for it?

* *What wounds did you bring to your marriage?*
* *How do you share your wounds, your pain with your God, your partner, and others?*

Growth takes place one day at a time.

More To Be Discovered

Most of us settle for far less than we are capable of having. Does this mean we are perfectly satisfied with the way things are?

A shot glass can only hold so much liquid. If more is placed in it, it will overflow. The capacity is limited by its size. A full size glass can hold more by comparison. It too, however, has its limited capacity. The issue is whether we are satisfied where we are in our growth life as a couple.

Have we reached our capacity? Is there more that we are capable of? More enjoyment, more love, and more happiness. If love is so important, are we fanning the fires of our relationship? Is one in the relationship eager for more and the other satisfied the way it is? This could pose a problem that requires some honest sharing and listening. The one who wants things just as they are needs to have an open mind while the other, who wants change, needs to learn patience and gentle persuasion.

* *What more is there to discover in your partner?*
* *How can you help each other in the pursuit of this daily discovery?*
* *How can you avoid taking each other for granted?*

Growth takes place one day at a time.

Love And Be Loved

What significant changes have you experienced in your personal life since you married? What attracted you to each other? What qualities that first attracted you to each other are still active? Was it love at first sight or was it a gradual, developing kind of process? Is it still going on? How are you handling the changes that have and still are occurring? What is challenging your marriage right now? Can you talk about it?

In spite of living in a world full of mechanical inventions and changing values and life styles, one dimension in your relationship does not change-the need to love and be loved. This need continues to exist in some form or degree. What light can you shed on these areas? Talk about it with each other and see where it takes you. This just may be what you need to spark you to more understanding and closeness in your relationship.

* *How is love expressed and received in your relationship?*
* *What changes have you made in these areas since you married?*

Growth takes place one day at a time.

Something Deeper Going On

"I don't know if we love each other anymore." "Our relationship is not what it was." "I am thinking of getting out of the marriage." These and others like them are statements often heard by a therapist. It isn't necessarily an issue of infidelity, abuse, or alcoholism. These can be expressions by one or both people in the relationship. They may be related to innocent experiences such as watching other couples hold hands or watching a movie on TV that starts memories of "it used to be that way, but it isn't now." These may bring a tear to the eye and a tug at the throat.

We may drift into wondering what our future will be like or if there will even be a future. That which brought us joy and hope may now find us "putting up" with each other. We may find ourselves joyless and cynical. We want to "fix it." That's great because it is a beginning but it will take time and some effort.

- *Is there any tentativeness in you regarding your commitment? If so, why? How?*
- *How can you use your doubts and uncertainties to help you discover your deeper needs and wants?*

Growth takes place one day at a time.

A Spiritual Connection

Looking at our partner and seeing more than meets the eye is a powerful force in our marriage. This calls for a spiritual outlook. It can deepen our love. This occurs when we recognize and admit that there is more to our spouse than we know or will ever know here on earth. We become partners with God in loving our partner.

We may belong to a group, such as a church or a synagogue. Perhaps, we may belong to some form of faith sharing group. This can also be helpful. We learn and receive encouragement from each other on our spiritual journey.

Make some time to share with each other in prayer. It need not to be formal. There are many things that we can pray for and making these known to each other can be enlightening and inspiring. Discuss the importance of this dimension in your life with each other.

• What does spirituality mean to you?
• Do you believe your maturity in spiritual matters has kept pace with your maturity in other areas of your life?
If so, how? If not, why not?

Growth takes place one day at a time.

Reinforce The Commitment

The beauty and comfort of a house is important but secondary to the structural strength of that house. Concentrating on the color of the walls or the location of the furniture is very secondary to how solid is the foundation. This is also true for your marriage.

You may need some work on your communication and other significant areas of your relationship but it is of primary importance that you look at your commitment to your relationship. Is it wobbly? Is is solid? Do you renew it from time to time? Are there any "if's" or "maybe's" that suggest some form of tentativeness in your relationship? If so, you need to confront them and meet them head on. If not, you still need to renew your commitment with each other. This does not simply mean a "grin and bear it" approach. It means you send a clear signal to each other that problems are expected and you choose to deal with them. The commitment remains intact. This occurs no matter how severe the emotional storm. Such commitment requires frequent and intentioned re-investment.

• What is the state of your marriage commitment
at this time in your life?
• How can you reinforce your commitment to each other?

Growth takes place one day at a time.

The Child Within

There is a little child in all of us. He or she may be happy and joyful, sad and insecure, angry and resentful, glad and hopeful. Where is your child these days?

Is your little child having fun with the little child in your partner? Do you do things with each other that are silly and good-natured? What are these fun things, and are you making time for fun and light living? This is an essential part of your life and your marriage. You cannot afford to leave your own natural child out of your marriage relationship. As you consider the importance of that little child within you, you may feel happy, sad, and even embarrassed over such a reference to yourself. The issue is your fun together.

How do you play together? Do you play? Be brave and discuss your playfulness in the light of the child within. Have fun doing it, please!

- *How much fun are you having with each other?*
- *What can you do to make this a priority?*
- *How can you help each other with this one?*

Growth takes place one day at a time.

Checking Things Out

Some of us have grown up in families where kissing, holding, and embracing was an expression of affection and was done naturally and spontaneously. For some of us that atmosphere was more formal and often distant. When we marry we experience ourselves settling into old and familiar structures. This is where we can help each other by our patience and our attempts to understand and appreciate each other's background.

Loving and sensitive expressions of affection need to be checked out with each other. Assumptions here are not necessarily helpful. Each one of us has a different understanding of closeness. We need to check out our likes and dislikes, our wants and our needs with each other. This helps prevent playing "psychiatrist" and lessens the risk of assuming your partner wishes and wants the same thing you do. Interpreting each other's wants in terms of affection is a delicate area. A review of this matter could bring some neat discoveries for both of you.

- *How can appreciation and understanding each other's background strengthen your relationship?*
- *In what specific areas could this be helpful to you and your partner?*

Growth takes place one day at a time.

The Responsibility Is Ours

Recently, a woman told me she purchased a new car. It was American-made. She is very conscious of promoting American-mades. In further listening, she said that the salesman impressed her so much with his smile and kind manner that she could not resist purchasing. This is a clear example of a responsive style of living and suggests the belief that the real source of power and influence lies outside of ourselves. This can lead to the simple belief that we hold others responsible for our happiness. It is common for such a belief to translate into statements such as, "he /she should make me happy."

The truth of the matter is that our happiness is really our responsibility. We can create the atmosphere for our partner to experience joy. As we strive to remain healthy and alive ourselves, we contribute to the well-being and joy of our partner.

- *What experiences in your relationship bring you happiness?*
- *What can you do to create an atmosphere of joy*
in your relationship?

Growth takes place one day at a time.

Appreciate What We Have

Often, we consider education as the process of taking in new information. This, of course, is true. In our marriage, we take in new information from the outside. There is, however, a natural rhythm, a pulse that is unique to each couple. This is why it is senseless to get caught up comparing our relationships with others. It is important that we look at our relationships in the light of their potential to become even more than they are now. Inherent in our relationships are all the basic ingredients to be happy and successful. These ingredients, of course, need nurturing and consistent attention.

What are you doing right now that is helpful for your relationship? What are the ways you show that you cherish and appreciate each other? Spend some time with this one and take heart.

• How can you bring out the best in each other?
• What little things are you doing each day to nurture the romance in your marriage?

Growth takes place one day at a time.

Understand Your Anger

In our arguments with each other, it is necessary to consider what is triggering the anger. Does it relate in any way to our need to be right? When this is our need, our perception of the reality is negatively affected. We can then believe it is necessary to stand on our own rights and granite-like position.

We tend to gather around ourselves those of like mind. Of course, there are always those around. They support our position and our anger. In fact, we can become so encouraged to stand up and justify our anger that it becomes difficult to even assess the meaning of it all. We may look around for someone who may report having experienced a similar situation. This adds to our justification for our feelings and our position.

Does your own internal peace mean anything? Consider seriously the question whether it is more important to be right than at peace within yourself. It's a question of perception. Where do you stand in all of this as an individual and as a couple?

- *Is it more important to be right than at peace within yourself?*
- *How does your answer affect your relationship?*

Growth takes place one day at a time.

Listen For The Signal

When I heard Barbara Streisand and Neil Diamond sing, "You don't bring me flowers anymore," I felt a tinge of guilt, and an awareness that perhaps my marriage needed a lift. What exactly that lift could be escaped me at the time. I was left simply with a desire to create a better marriage. The truth is that little remembrances are not limited to special occasions. It may be something other than a flower, but the thought of being thoughtful rang true and I began to consider in just what ways I show my partner that I love her. There are different and unique ways we can show our love. Perhaps, an open sharing of what we would like from each other would help. This need not take away from our creativity and efforts to surprise each other. The important thing is that we recognize how often there are little reminders like the songs we hear that can nudge us on our way.

> • *What are some of the unique experiences in your life that nudge you to value your partner?*
> • *What are the different and unique ways you show your love to each other?*

Growth takes place one day at a time.

Let Your Response Be Clear

Most of us are generous with other people, including members of our own family. Along with this attractive quality comes the natural expectations by others that we will always be generous and available. We seem to take on a reputation that entitles others to rely upon this generosity. We volunteer to help out on a church or school project and the assumption is that we are available for the next one. People call us with innocent requests and we need to be able to say "yes" or "no" to those requests. For some of us this is difficult.

We need to recognize the importance of having control over our responses and evaluate them in the light of having a necessary balance. This can apply to the assumptions we make of each other in our marriages and families. As much as we might protest and register our dislike, we may unwittingly be teaching each other how to continue unnecessary assumptions and demands upon each other.

- *When do you feel you are taken for granted and even taken advantage of?*
- *How do your activities and responses teach others to read you wrongly?*

Growth takes place one day at a time.

Be Prepared To Live Alone

Old slogans have a tendency to hang on. Especially those that assign tasks such as, "you belong at work," "you belong at home." Not all of us are truly "liberated." We all have our internal messages. Some of us feel threatened with equality in our relationships. This, even though we are living in modern times.

If you are married for twenty or thirty years, how have you prepared for each other's departure? Ordinarily, a woman's life expectancy is eight to ten years longer. We are all living longer, but we all have to die. We had best be ready by acquiring the necessary emotional, intellectual, spiritual, and social skills. We need to be ready to stand alone. We need to know the "ins" and "outs" of everyday life. Home maintenance, finances, taxes, car maintenance, insurance, etc.

How can you obtain the emotional support you need when loss occurs with friends, family, job, or volunteer work? Set some time aside to talk this one over. Make it a double session. Plan some specific action as a result of your sharing and review later.

- *What picture do you have for your relationship in your older years?*
- *How are you helping each other prepare for your future together and alone?*

Growth takes place one day at a time.

A Compromise May Be Needed

In our marriage, we cannot always line up on one side fully. The bad or the good, the right or the wrong, the black or the white. The gray or the middle, or somewhere in between is COMPROMISE. This does not mean we have sold out, abandoned ship, nor does it signify a wimpy posture.

We can look at several possibilities. In a given situation, we can find ourselves in a kind of cold war effort. We are at an impasse. We can't seem to go one way or the other. Another possibility is, we give here and receive something there. It is not a one-sided deal. Each of us wins and loses together. Advantage, both. Another is, we really want to compromise providing, of course, it goes one way—our way. This is a one-sided attempt to control and does not result in promoting the welfare of the marriage.

- *Where, if at all, does compromise fit into your marriage?*
- *How flexible can you be without giving up your beliefs and position on issues of importance to you and your relationship?*

Growth takes place one day at a time.

Be True To Yourself

We are not always sure of ourselves. We look to others to supply answers for our needs and uncertainties. Our identity, who we are, and what we believe about ourselves, is crucial to understand. This is no easy task, but it can be done. Slowly, of course, but it can be done.

It takes courage to evaluate our beliefs about ourselves and the world in which we live, especially as we get older. We get set in our ways of perceiving. It is usually when something isn't working well in our lives that brings us closer to wanting to learn.

Perhaps a simple example here might be helpful. Ask yourself if you can act the same when you are at home, at work, with friends. Are you the same person, and do you adjust merely to the different circumstances? Do you act differently when you are alone, together with your partner, and with friends or other couples?

- *How much confidence do you have in yourself?*
- *What can you do to help raise the confidence in each other?*

Growth takes place one day at a time.

We All Hurt Sometime

All of us have been hurt in one way or another. We can't live our lives without being hurt or hurting someone, often unintentionally. They may seem cool toward us, meanwhile, an emotional barrier goes up. There may be a guarded response, or the person may stay away from us. A disharmony occurs in our relationships when we feel we have been hurt. We may hurt someone else with what we say or do. Sometimes, we handle our hurt with tolerance, humility, understanding, or generous overlooking.

There are hurts that cut deeply. This occurs usually with significant people in our lives, such as parents, partners, relatives, etc. These require our forgiveness. Our past is a segment of our history.

• What are the hurts in your life?
• Can you identify those that need forgiveness?

Growth takes place one day at a time.

The Time Is Now

Today, we are here. Tomorrow, well, it has not yet come. Some of us plan very well for our future. We even set aside what we could enjoy right now so that we can do a better job of it sometime down the line. We forfeit the present moment. And yet, it is this present moment that is all we really have. One of us may get ill or lose the desire to do what seemed exciting and attractive at one time. We may be of the belief that we should wait until we have more money or just the right situation. All of these can hinder us from utilizing the current moment to its fullest.

Are you respectful of the present moment? Are you putting off to tomorrow or next week what you could be enjoying alone or together right now? Is it a trip, a sport, a task? Talk it over. Why not now? Enjoy each moment. It is all you have. The past is gone. The future is not yet here. Now is the time to enjoy—to live.

• *How could respect for the present moment contribute to the joy you experience in your relationship?*

Growth takes place one day at a time.

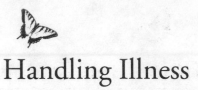

Handling Illness

No one is immune from illness. We all get sick. Often seriously, and it may mean hospitalization or bed confinement for a time. We may have a lingering illness or the one-day flu.

Is your caring limited to a few words of inquiring how the other is feeling and leave it at that? How is illness handled in your family? How was illness handled when you were growing up? Who paid attention to you when you became ill, and how was that attention and concern expressed? Was it expressed at all? Were you simply left alone? Did you prefer to be alone? Are there any similarities with the way illness is treated in your current relationship? We tend to imitate past experiences.

*•How do you treat each other when one of you is ill
or just not feeling well?*
*• Do your spiritual values have a bearing on the way
you handle illness? If so, how? If not, why not?*

Growth takes place one day at a time.

Consider Your Perception

The world, for some, is a scary place to be. It appears threatening and ready to attack us. Of course, we really are talking of how we perceive others in our world. All of us grow up adding lenses to our vision of the world. Some of us have more, some less. Some strong, some weak. Some accurate, some distorted. We carry those lenses into our marriage.

When we perceive our partner on the attack, perhaps, through yelling or some other means, it is difficult to not want to defend ourselves. This creates a distance, at least, temporarily. But, if we can see beyond that apparent attack and recognize the hurt or the fear underneath, our experience can be quite different. We can experience ourselves reaching out instead of pulling back. We can train ourselves to look for the fear that covers up the love. It is a question of how we perceive. The easiest, at first, is to go with what we first see.

> • *Is there any one predominant feeling at the time of the conflict with your partner?*
> • *How could your perception of the events involved be contributing to that feeling?*

Growth takes place one day at a time.

No Fault Relationship

In every relationship we have to face the unexpected. Things go wrong and things get difficult. We need to meet these challenges head on as a team. Blaming someone else makes this all the more difficult. When you blame, you place the cause at your partner's feet. Your understanding of the situation may be right on, but blaming your partner can be destructive. When you blame your partner for something you are responsible for, you deny your responsibility. You shelter yourself in a lie. When you blame yourself as a lead in to really blaming your partner, this also can be destructive. "I really goofed... I should have known better than to believe you could be relied on to balance the checkbook".

Take back your blame and look for solutions. Look for ways you could limit the situation from occurring in the future. This is a very constructive way of strengthening your relationship. At those time when your partner is at fault, offer support and an effort to deal with these situations. Remember, we are looking for two winners - not a winner and a looser.

- *How and when does blame occur in your relationship?*
- *What can you do personally to avoid blame?*
- *What are the benefits from having a no fault relationship?*

Growth takes place one day at a time.

Programming Your Love

It is difficult to admit that in some way we may be keeping score of what our partner does or does not do for us. We all enter marriage with a set of expectations that we simply believe "must" be fulfilled if we are ever going to be happy. We find ways to send messages to our partner as to how he or she should and even must, behave toward us. It may reach the intensity of a demand. This can foster a lot of frictions and unhappiness.

We may not be aware of how we attempt to program our partner to fit into our set of expectations. Our partner may try to accommodate our expectations and fail because he or she has never dealt with these realistically. Our love can come under suspicion of being conditional. Consider your relationship in the light of the expectations you have of each other. This could be helpful in your efforts to clarify your expectations of each other.

- *Are you keeping score of your partner's efforts to make you happy?*
- *How realistic are your expectations of each other in light of such a score card?*

Growth takes place one day at a time.

Be At Peace

Seeking peace and tranquility by having God in our lives and in our relationships, is held suspect by some people. It is difficult for some to believe that God, the Almighty Giver, would be so lovingly interested in our happiness and well-being. After all, they say, isn't this a dependent position of a weakling and isn't that totally unrealistic? No, of course not. This is one vision of God. A vision that carries a distorted view of a loving Creator. This view, unfortunately, seeps down into our visions of life and the world and ourselves. It contains a view of the world as mean and terribly unfair. Relationships are made to be broken and love is something you read about or dream about but never expect to have. Are these views in any way familiar to you? Do you really believe in God's design for you to be happy?

> • *Does your vision of your God foster peace*
> *and tranquility in your life and relationship?*
> • *How does this vision of God affect*
> *your relationship spiritually?*

Growth takes place one day at a time.

Attend To Your Own Garden

Does it bother you that others have more than you? Perhaps more money, a larger and more luxurious house, a nicer car, more talent, a happier marriage? These are just a few examples to make the point. Can you identify related feelings such as envy or jealousy? We may feel that God plays favorites. Some of our friends lead lives no different from us and are somehow doing better and seem happier. It is tough to say, "let God and let go."

We cannot see some of the important aspects of life with our eyes alone. There are some things hidden from us, especially some things we may not be able to read in the faces and lives of others. We have our own gardens to watch and nurture. Are you doing that?

• How are you concentrating to make your marriage very special?
• Where does God fit in your marriage?

Growth takes place one day at a time.

Be Open To Healing

We hear and read a lot about healing. Often, it is in the context of a marriage relationship. This can be an enlightening, though painful, experience. We discover how easy, and even automatic, it is to blame the world outside of us for our pain and misfortune. It is difficult to shift our attitudes from blame and shame to understanding and acceptance. In our marriages we can justify our anger or resentment by simply avoiding our contribution to the situation. We can set our sights on what is wrong or broken and pass the opportunity to heal and move on.

Can you assess your need to blame and uncover your deeper need to let go of your hurts and perceived injustices? What can you do to shift your attitude to one of acceptance and look for ways to trust in each other's goodwill and inner innocence? It is a task worth your effort. Consider the implications for yourself and your marriage.

- *What needs to be healed in your life?*
- *What needs to be healed in your marriage?*

Growth takes place one day at a time.

Take Courage

Sometimes it's hard not to just give up. Resign ourselves to the inevitable. Throw in the towel. We gave it our best shot. We gave it time. At one time or another we all feel victimized, defeated, and depressed. The seeds of positive thoughts and feelings seem to have betrayed us. We need to recognize our moods for what they are and believe that they will pass. Trouble does not go on forever.

The stage is set to decide in favor of a good talk with ourselves. It may be time for a pep talk, a visit with a friend who will not only listen attentively but will also give us some honest feedback. This may be the time when we can accept where we really are in our lives, and know that each day is filled with its own opportunity for suffering, joy, and awakening. Be sure to look at this day as special. Whatever your mood, no matter how busy, whisper an encouraging word to yourself and your partner. Each day is a new beginning. This can be yours.

- *What in your relationship needs to be faced with courage?*
- *How can you encourage and be encouraged today?*

Growth takes place one day at a time.

Encouragement To Love

The first school of learning how to love and be loved was in our homes growing up. If the words "I love you" were seldom used or heard, if hugs and kisses were not experienced, then, chances are, we will continue this pattern. If feelings were freely expressed and attention readily given and received, then we are more apt to express our feelings with trust and confidence.

Whatever your experience, you can learn to love and express your love. This is a basic need for all of us. You may have to unlearn the old beliefs and behaviors that keep you from experiencing the wonderful fruits of your efforts to love and be loved in return. It may seem awkward at first, but with encouragement and loving understanding, you can help yourself and each other express your deepest need to love and be loved.

- *How do you express love to your partner?*
- *How does your partner express his or her love to you?*

Growth takes place one day at a time.

Time Alone–Time Together

In our marriage, we need time alone and time together. This natural process exists in every marriage, and needs our attention. As a process, it never goes away nor is it ever completely solved. This is the salt and pepper of your marriage.

Of course, you feel a lot better and more comfortable if both of you prefer the same closeness and distance. Are there any of us who have not requested some time alone and received a disappointed look or comment? Is there any one of us who has not proclaimed our need for time to be together only to find the other is quite comfortable being alone or separate? We grow in our ability to accommodate each other without giving up our own identity.

Your relationship, in order to be alive and growing, is constantly changing. It is not stagnant. You can come to realize that a satisfied partner is really essential to your marriage.

> • *How do you make time for yourself?*
> • *How do you make time to be together?*

Growth takes place one day at a time.

Monitoring What You Believe

Consider monitoring what comes into your mind as well as your body. We are often very careful about our food intake—what we eat and drink. We are not as careful about what we take into our marriage, whether it is by way of television, books, films, etc.

Our beliefs are formed early in life. We maintain or rid ourselves of these beliefs, depending on whether or not they promote our daily peace of mind and happiness. Most of us need to make conscious, willful decisions each day. Old negative beliefs and attitudes go away slowly. They like to linger on safely tucked away, only to rise and influence our thoughts and feelings another time.

How much do your beliefs and attitudes influence the way you live? This depends upon how aware you are of yourself and the people you live with. Today is a good time to consider some of the major influences in your life. What are they, and how do they affect you personally, and your marriage?

> • *How have your beliefs about marriage changed since you married?*
> • *Have these changes influenced your relationship positively or negatively?*

Growth takes place one day at a time.

Taking Charge With Love

When we accept responsibility for our own lives, our marriage, the thoughts we have, our feelings and intentions, then blame loses its appeal and power. Taking charge of our lives does not mean we run roughshod over others. It means that we stop looking for excuses for our behavior and come to grips with what we want our lives and relationships to be.

Love can become our prime motivation. It is really the essence of our being anyway. When we recognize that our love can conquer fear and any other hindrance to our happiness, we come in contact with the very source of all love in the world. We experience ourselves connected to all that is living and beautiful around us. We share unconditional love with each other.

> • *How can taking charge of your life strengthen your love for each other?*
> • *How is personal responsibility encouraged, nurtured and rewarded in your relationship?*

Growth takes place one day at a time.

Choose Living This Day

It is difficult to steer the course of our day without looking ahead or behind. We can feel pulled from both directions. The fact of the matter is that we have only today, this day, to live our life. We will no doubt face situations we have not chosen to face. These will all be unplanned. Or we may walk the same road we did yesterday and all may seem so familiar.

The fact is, however, this is a new day with a new heart. We can dedicate this day to peace of mind and to the happiness at heart. Old memories and hurts, broken promises, and sincere efforts are left unclaimed. From these, we can learn. Today, we can call upon the powerful resources of our will and our dedications to living this day, not in fear but in love and hope. This is our choice. What will it be? When we choose love today, we can be at peace. This will surely affect our relationships with others this day.

• How can today be a new beginning for you?
• What effect could this have on your relationship?

Growth takes place one day at a time.

Message Heard Is Message Sent

Love and compassion can sometimes be expressed in ways that are difficult to accept and understand. There are times when we may need to advise our partner regarding a certain behavior. In our experiences, we may believe that a certain behavior is harmful to our marriage. If we express ourselves in a loving and direct way, it may cause some pain or fear. The harsh truth in such an instance may have nothing to do with the truth. It may have more to do with the tone of our voice and how our partner experiences the truth being presented.

If we experience ourselves open to learning from each other, we can be more accepting when our partner tells us something that is difficult to swallow. Share with each other the ways you help each other deal with the behaviors you have difficulty with in your relationship.

- *With what accuracy are messages sent and received in your relationship?*
- *How do you share and check your meaning with each other?*

Growth takes place one day at a time.

A Learning Experience

We all can pretty much agree that problems and conflicts are going to occur in our relationships. These same problems can occur over and over again, sometimes wearing different faces, shapes and forms. This occurs because they simply have not been resolved and they keep popping up. There is something to learn here. Our goal can be the ability to set the problem or conflict out in front of us. We have a problem. We are not the problem. This mind set takes time and patience to achieve.

Our relationship takes on a new power when we join forces and unite our energies, goodwill and skills. We return to the scene of our argument after ventilating our feelings and we are able to ask ourselves and each other, "What happened?" This is a very powerful way of nurturing and growing our lives together. We are taking responsibility for what is happening and we are responding with creative solutions. This moves us off the blaming and on to productive learning. We are giving a realistic direction for our hopes and goodwill.

- *What conflicts and problems surface regularly in your relationship?*
- *How can you provide for an ongoing dialogue and discussion of your differences?*

Growth takes place one day at a time.

Turn On To Aliveness

There are a variety of reasons for experiencing boredom in marriage. One of these is the lack of challenge. We may want peace at all costs. There is an appearance of tranquility. No ruffles or rough spots. This is not always the best thing for a relationship. On the other hand, to have a relationship that is chaotic, unpredictable, and explosive may be interesting and even fascinating to watch, but should never be imitated. So, we want to avoid moving too far to one side or the other.

We need to stimulate each other, to challenge each other. New ideas, new interests, new suggestions provide a necessary variety and an invitation to aliveness. It sharpens us and arouses a new flow of life in us and in our relationship. Of course, this can be a little on the scary side especially if this is new for you. Be aware of your need to stimulate, and turn your partner on and away from dullness in your relationship. Be creative in your sharing.

• *How can you challenge each other?*

Growth takes place one day at a time.

The Movement In Your Relationship

What are some significant changes you have noticed in yourself and in your partner since marriage? This may take a little while. Just a reminder that we do not freeze our identity at any one point along the way. We may have sought psychotherapy, had a severe illness, experienced some form of religious conversion, or some experience that has made one or both partners much different than when we were first married. When we acknowledge the impact of our experiences, we recognize that our growth as a couple is never static. Therefore, it is impossible to predict what we will be as a couple years down the line.

Ideally, we are merging into a union that is accenting our similarities. In the beginning, opposites may attract, but it is our similarities that enable us to move more evenly in the direction of mutuality. Consider the movement in your identity as a couple.

- *What personal changes have you made that satisfy you?*
- *Have these changes moved you closer to each other? How?*

Growth takes place one day at a time.

Compatible Values

Values such as trust and loyalty, religious and moral beliefs are of significant importance to most of us. They come up more often than we acknowledge or are even aware of. When we share a common value system, we reduce a significant amount of tension in our marriage. When there is a serious difference or conflict involving our honesty or ethical position, we need to have frequent communication about the issues involved. This could result from experiencing different backgrounds that make our views and beliefs strongly incompatible.

Our need then is to note these differences and find ways to deal with each other respectfully and openly. Religious conflicts can occur and they can raise feelings that test our skills to communicate. Discuss your values with each other and how compatible you are regarding these values.

- *What values are important to you?*
- *How have these values influenced your marriage?*

Growth takes place one day at a time.

Give Yourself A Break

How often lately have your thoughts turned to vacationing? Some sort of break, a respite, getting away from it all. We all need a time out–a change of scenery. They can turn up as "mental health days," "a step in the sunshine." Whatever we call them, we need to recognize and listen to the call of our bodies, our feelings, our needs and wants.

We may drive ourselves and then feel the tension and the pressure. These can be times of breaking down and breaking out. It may mean a simple minute break, or a change of scenery for a day or two. It may suggest the need for a realistic assessment of where you are and where you are going alone and together. This is no easy task especially for those of us who drive ourselves hard.

- *How do you know when you need a break?*
- *What are you doing about it, alone and together?*

Growth takes place one day at a time.

Confirm Each Other

We all need to be confirmed. This raises our self-esteem and makes us feel good about ourselves. In addition, we need someone to confirm what we are already doing. This tells us we are on the right track. It may not seem like a big deal, but it is important to have our efforts recognized and confirmed. We all need assurance. We need to hear it from our partner, that what we are doing is right on target, that our judgment is good.

This may not change our direction, but it can move us from a state of doubt to feeling more assured, and that can be helpful. When you check out your actions or your intentions to do something, and you hear a positive confirmation from your partner, is this helpful to you? Check on how you confirm each other.

- *How can confirmation increase your self-esteem and make you feel good about yourself?*
- *Identify the ways you like this confirmation to be given and received in your relationship.*

Growth takes place one day at a time.

Keep Your Sense Of Humor

When was the last time you had a good belly laugh? Not just a "ha ha," controlled and muffled. Do you remember how you felt? Were you exhilarated? It works magic. It turns up the inner juices. How do you rate the humor in your life, marriage, and family? There are times, of course, when we all have to be serious. But is there a balance?

Are you looking for fun times, and what are these for you? If there is an absence of fun times in our lives, then something very valuable and needed is missing. Humor is a powerful force. It can affect our attitude and disposition in a major way. It gets us through daily scrapes and bruises. It is excellent for mind, body, and soul. Consider who and what makes you really laugh. Uncover the humor and fun resources in your marriage. You will be doing something neat and powerful for yourself and your relationship.

> • *Is there enough laughter in your life?*
> • *How are you having fun together?*

Growth takes place one day at a time.

I'm Right... So What?

We all have our convictions. But, convictions need to be open to new data or else we can become rigid and closed minded. In the heat of a battle, when our ego appears on the line, proving we are right fuels a competitive struggle. The issue then becomes - I am right and you are wrong. Is it really worth the risk of alienating your partner so as to be right and diminish your partner in the process? This can hardly ever replace your efforts to exchange idea's, as strong and certain as you may feel.

There are times when your issue is a big one, like the decision to have major surgery. Whether a blue paint is better than beige may be significant but hardly fits into the serious category. You can be right and still recognize the validity of your partner's position. Your need to be right and your efforts to prove it could be a dead end road. In short, you could be right and yet be dead wrong. You may choose to give up your right in a given instance for the sake of furthering the peace and harmony in your relationship. In an intimate relationship we need to be ready to forego our need to be right.

- *How open are you to the ever occurring new data coming into your life and relationship?*
- *How active are the issues of who's right and who's wrong, in your relationship?*
- *What could you do to promote greater acceptance of each other beliefs, thoughts and feelings?*

Growth takes place one day at a time.

Listen For Your Name

What's in a name? Well, for some, it's a kind of face whereby we are known. It tells the world who we are. Shakespeare asked, "What is in a name? That which we call a rose, by any other name would smell as sweet." Goethe said, "A man's name is a perfectly fitting garment, which like the skin, has grown over him, at which one cannot rake and scrape without injuring the man himself." Our name is our very private possession.

In the Bible, Isaiah speaks of a loving God who calls us by name and tells us how precious we are. There are courses being taught that demonstrate ways we can learn to remember names because when we do, we pay tribute to the person we meet and this is a very strong affirmation of that person.

Take time to close your eyes now and repeat your own name slowly. Listen for the sound as you call out your name.

• As a couple, listen to each other as you speak your own names. Call each other by name...slowly...reverently...softly...lovingly.

Growth takes place one day at a time.

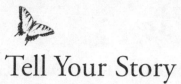

Tell Your Story

Everyone likes stories. There are even groups that meet on occasion to tell stories and consider various ways one can be an effective storyteller. We all have our own special story to tell and we need others to listen to our story.

Can you share your story with your partner? Perhaps you have certain events in your life that have caused you much pain, sadness and sorrow. Those experiences may even be influencing your life in different ways now. There are also happy events and joy-filled experiences you have had. There are customs and practices you also have experienced and all are a part of your story.

Do you take the time to share your story with your children? It would be unfortunate for you to die and leave your story untold. Begin slowly but do begin. Share your story and listen to each other. Begin today.

* *How could you share the unfolding of your marriage story with each other? With other important people in your life?*

Growth takes place one day at a time.

Reach Out To Others

By reading or listening to these daily reflections you indicate that you want to grow as a person and as a couple. You may be searching for specific help in a certain area of your life and marriage. Whatever your reason, be aware today of how you and your partner relate to others. These others can be existing friends, other members of your church, community, business or neighborhood. Are you mostly by yourselves or are both of you making efforts to reach out to others?

For some of us, reaching out is difficult. We would not refuse to help another but we have difficulty reaching out. We consider that to be pushy, aggressive, or even snoopy.

As a couple, consider your efforts to make friends, and not let your fears prevent you from allowing others to get to know you. Talk to each other about the experiences you have in this area of your life together.

- *What are you doing right now to nurture the relationships you already have?*
- *What can you do as a couple to reach out to others this week?*

Growth takes place one day at a time.

Listen To The Rhythm

What counts most for you in your life right now? Is it difficult to prioritize your needs, your wants, your values?

Often, we move from one event to another, from one experience to another, and we seem to take no notice of any particular movement or rhythm. What importance does this day have for you? Perhaps, it might help if you stopped yourself long enough to have just a minute break from the usual pace. Listen to your heartbeat. Listen to the noise. Listen to the silence. Listen to your thoughts and how they come and go so rapidly. Take the moment to pay attention to you. Rejoice and be glad in you.

> • *Is there a calm or turmoil in your life right now?*
> • *What forms the rhythm in your marriage?*

Growth takes place one day at a time.

Do Your Thing

In our relationships we are not always on the same page. We experience disagreement over who does what, for how long and at what time. This may be a time for some new understanding, negotiations, clarifications and even some sort of compromise.

When you are at odds with your partner's choice, you could be faced with a common dilemma. How strong are you in your position? Can you even feel entitled to your position? What is your need at the time? Can you postpone your need in java of your partner's satisfaction? You may have the tendency to overcompromise, to overplease and deprive yourself of a simple pleasure.

We all need to experience a proportionate give and receive. One sided support and overcompromising by one partner needs a good review. Doing your own thing can sometimes cause inconvenience but not necessarily signal willful neglect. Experiencing mild inconvenience and discomfort while supporting your partner is a loving way to strengthen your relationship.

- *What are some of your pet projects and activities?*
- *How do you receive support and encouragement for these activities?*
- *How can doing your own thing become a plus and not a negative in your relationship?*

Growth takes place one day at a time.

Name Your Feelings

We seldom live our lives in a straight line. We go through ups and downs. We are not going to be euphoric all the time, nor will we be depressed and sullen all the time. We strive for a happy medium. We try to catch the ebb and flow of life and hopefully discover our own wonderful rhythms. We do this not only personally, but in our marriage as well.

What brings you pain, sadness, stress and what seems to give you pleasure, joy, and contentment? It is important to name these, to identify and call them by name. They will then not become strangers or intruders but rather events and reactions that you can embrace with your awareness and then you can recognize them for what they are. Pay attention to these rhythms in your own life and in your marriage. These can be fruitful blessings for you and your marriage.

- *What feelings are most noticeably expressed in your marriage?*
- *What importance is there in owning your feelings as opposed to attributing them to outside sources?*

Growth takes place one day at a time.

We Can Make It Happen

Good results flow from positive expectations. You expect that you can get through your problems, obstacles and the difficult times that cast shadows over your relationship. Your relationship does not need the pessimistic expectations attached to such slogans as, "it isn't going to work," "it's just a matter of time," "we're never going to make it together," "you're going to find someone else anyway." Within your expectations there lies the element of predictability, especially when your expectations are negative and pessimistic.

This can become more complicated when you intend to remain in the relationship and you continue on with your negative expectations, needs and desires. Choose to verbalize positive expectations. This is a powerful force in your relationship. When you nurture your intentions and expectations for a successful and satisfying relationship, and you continue to acquire the necessary skills to make this happen, then you are making it happen. You are not just leaving it to chance.

• Are you aware of any negative or pessimistic messages you are sending to your partner?
• How strong are your desire and intentions to make things happen in your relationship?
Growth takes place one day at a time.

Expressing Your Generosity

Generosity is often linked with giving to the have nots. It passes off as sharing of our bounty, and as Americans we can embrace the belief that we need to continue to be a generous people. This generosity continues to be challenged daily by our own increasing awareness of the poverty around us. This is happening to us with greater frequency as we learn of children without food and adults with little to bear the day. We can easily succumb to the numbing thought that we are just individuals in this vast sea of need. Looking the other way, however, leaves us with no less a desperate image of who the poor and needy are.

"Humanitarianism is a link that binds together all Americans. Whenever tragedy or disaster has struck in any corner of the world, the American people have promptly and generously extended their hand of mercy and help. Generosity has never impoverished the giver—it has enriched the lives of those who have practiced it." - Dwight D. Eisenhower.

> • *How do you express your generosity?*
> • *With whom do you share your bounty?*

Growth takes place one day at a time.

Valuing Each Other

"We must never undervalue any person. The workman does not have his or her work despised in his presence. Now God is present everywhere and every person is his work." - Desales.

Can you recognize the good actions of others? We all seek to be valued. When we do not feel valued by another, we feel hurt and angry. To practice giving appreciation is truly a generous and virtuous act. In addition, the giver receives great satisfaction and a sense of well-being.

Can you appreciate the uniqueness and specialness your partner possesses? Do you recognize these gifts but seldom, if ever, express your recognition? Look for the good, the sacred. It is always there waiting to be recognized and responded to. We are gifts to each other.

- *How do you express appreciation to your partner?*
- *How do you feel when you experience yourself valued by your partner?*

Growth takes place one day at a time.

Rest in Your God

At the end of this day we may discover that events did come and go. Perhaps, the control we had over them now seems to suggest that not much of what happened followed any particular plan. Our awareness of who is really in control may remind us of a higher power that moves and sustains our world.

"Look at the beautiful butterfly and learn from it to trust in God. One might wonder where it could live in tempestuous nights, in the whirlwind or in the stormy day; but I have noticed it is safe and dry under the broad leaf while rivers have been flooded and the mountain oaks torn up from their roots." - Jeremy Taylor.

Every so often we can feel the trusting hand of our God as we experience our need to seek shelter from the frenzy, the unsettling events of the day. Take those minutes to be calm and feel sheltered. "Be still and know that I am God."

- *Where do you go for shelter when the storms occur in your life?*
- *When are those times that you most experience the presence of your God?*

Growth takes place one day at a time.

Recognize Your Higher Power

Just how much control over our lives do we really have? Victor Frankl, the well-known psychiatrist confined to a concentration camp, decided that his captors and torturers had control over his mobility but not over his freedom. They could not get to that internal freedom no matter what they decided to do to him.

We may not be faced with such confinement, but we do face events and circumstances that demand our response. It may be a death, a catastrophe, a disease, a loss of a job or any set of circumstances that we have to face. Is your response one of throwing up your hands in despair and futility? Do you place it all in God's hands, call it all divine providence, totally beyond you, and leave it at that?

- *When is it that you decide to ask God to take over and you believe that it is out of your hands?*
- *How does your partner share in your experience?*

Growth takes place one day at a time.

Giving Each Other Reassurance

There are moments in our lives when we need support and reassurance from each other. It doesn't mean that we are helpless or incapable. We need, however, to know and identify just what forms that reassurance should take. Would it be best to experience it in terms of being listened to, a caring look, a holding of the hand, a word of approval or encouragement? This is important because once we identify what we want we increases the chances that we will get what we need. It also makes it easier on the person who is asked since it is clear what is wanted.

When you seek reassurance, you are seeking a vote of confidence from the person you look to for support. We need to reassure each other that while we cannot read the future or control the present, we can be there for each other, cheering and encouraging each other on. Practice asking for and giving reassurance to each other.

- *In what area of your life right now do you most need reassurance from your partner?*
- *How would you like that reassurance given to you?*

Growth takes place one day at a time.

April 14

The Children in Their Place

Our children are a special blessing and joy. They should never be placed in a position to fulfill us or become the main source for improving an already difficult marriage. We must avoid any conscious or unconscious need to experience through our children what was denied to us as children.

They need to know we will never let them assume roles that belong to us as adults. It is inappropriate for us to use our children as intermediaries, part-time confidants and transmitters of communications.

Look again at your relationship with your children and consider the many blessings and joys they are for you. Perhaps a family meeting just to express appreciation and positive feelings would be helpful at this time.

• Name the blessings your children bring to you.
• If you have no children, name the people in your life who are a blessing to you.

Growth takes place one day at a time.

Open to the Truth

Facing the truth about ourselves is seldom easy, especially when it is told to us by another. Perhaps one of the reasons for this is that our own personal awareness of ourselves is lacking. We tend to protect ourselves through denial, ignorance, and simple avoidance. Yet, this could be one of the most helpful aids in the journey of personal and marriage growth.

When your partner draws attention to something you have done or said, do you want to defend yourself because it is difficult to admit personal ownership? This need not be an indication of a permanent flaw. Most often we fall into a rhythm we are comfortable with and in a given situation we may respond in a defensive way.

- *Are you open to what your partner sees in you?*
- *Can you go beyond your immediate need to protect yourself and see if there is any truth in what he/she says?*

Growth takes place one day at a time.

Some Inspired Thoughts

In reading from The Book of Tobit in the Old Testament, I reflected on several thoughts. One, how important it is for those of us who are married to perceive ourselves in solidarity with other married couples. We are bound to each other in a unique way. We are able to touch other couples around us through our own openness, struggles and accomplishments.

Another is that like Tobias we need to be firm in our convictions, undaunted in our pursuit of what we believe. When faced with obstacles and seeming overwhelming odds, we do what we believe we have to do and stay with our convictions and beliefs.

The other thought was of the importance of placing ourselves in the hands of a higher power, our God. Along with Sarah and Tobias, we commit ourselves and our families to a continued deep faith and trust in our God. "Grant that we may grow old together."

> • *What resources do you go to for inspiration?*
> *For yourself and your marriage?*
> • *How are you special resources of inspiration for each other?*

Growth takes place one day at a time.

The Way We Communicate

When we consider the way we communicate with each other, we may realize that our difficulties do not arise from deception or ill will. Often, we have to remind ourselves and each other that what we say is not what is heard and what is heard is often not what is said. We come from different backgrounds and we learn to label things differently. What we consider "neat" or "good" receives a different definition from our partner. What we learned growing up to be acceptable and even desired, our partner may have learned to be unacceptable and should be shunned.

Are there any gestures or mannerisms you notice accompanying certain feelings or beliefs? Certain gestures are understood to indicate certain specific moods or feelings. After some years of marriage, we gain an understanding of our mutual labeling system. It could be helpful to share what these are in your relationship.

- *How are the messages you send to each other checked
for accuracy and understanding?*
- *What have you learned about each other's unique labeling
system?*

Growth takes place one day at a time.

Communicating Responsibly

Assuming responsibility for our thoughts, feelings, and behavior is a strong indication of maturity. It contributes immensely to personal growth and a sense of high self-esteem. When I can say, "I feel," "I think," "I want," these help me express my own personal awareness in an assertive and responsible way.

It is, however, also important to know that if our conversations with each other contain only "I don't," " I always," "I'd rather not," I, I, I, then there may just be too many "I's" and not enough "we's." Listening to ourselves and each other can help us check out where "we are" in our marriage as well as where "I am." Building a "we" takes time, energy, and hard work even though we realize how naturally important it is to us to relate closely to each other. Check your pronouns and share your results with each other.

> • *How can you promote the "we" in your marriage
> without losing the "I"?*
> • *How can you encourage responsible communication
> in your marriage?*

Growth takes place one day at a time.

Your Happiness

Happiness is defined in many different ways. The theologian, the philosopher, the poet, the musician, each considers it to be a process and an end product. To reach or seek it directly is to leave us grasping for the air.

To search for the ingredients special to ourselves is both hard work and often a mysterious journey. It seems to involve a deep sense of security. We know who we are at a given moment in time. We advance to a sense of separateness and our self-esteem is intact. We come to experience our feelings matching our heart. What comes from our lips is really what we think and feel at the time. We feel a sense of integrity. We can bring joy to each other naturally because there is an openness to give and receive that joy. We affirm and feel affirmed. This is all possible and worthwhile striving for. It is our happiness.

- *What gives you the most happiness in your marriage?*
- *How can you both increase the happiness in your marriage?*

Growth takes place one day at a time.

Celebrate You

Today may or may not be your birthday. In either case, let's consider the way we celebrate our own lives. Can you celebrate you?

A newborn draws our attention immediately and easily. We may say or hear someone near us say, "Isn't she cute?" "Look at that face," "How beautiful, how precious." What happens when we grow up? We become just one of the run of the mill people. What is currently preventing us from simply looking in the mirror and saying softly, "You are precious, you are a real gem, you are special, you are really neat."

Are you crying right now, smiling happily, or skeptical because you no longer know how to celebrate your life? Can you acknowledge God's hand in this? Read Psalm 139 and share with your partner.

- *What are some ways you can celebrate you?*
- *What are some ways you can celebrate each other?*

Growth takes place one day at a time.

Stay With Honest Intentions

It is difficult at times not to become discouraged, hurt, and angry when our best intentions are undermined and our overtures to another are rejected. We find it easy to personalize these situations. It is as if we offered a part of ourselves and when we experience the unexpected response, we may feel like a part of ourselves is lost. We must not allow ourselves, however, to become overly upset. We may need to realize that we made the offer honestly and with our best intention.

We do not have control over other people's responses. We may need "to shake the dust from our feet" when our efforts to bring a blessing to someone fall on deaf ears. The very ones that we expect to understand and support us are the ones who often are the last to respond and may have difficulty with our actions. We need to be convinced ourselves that we are on the right track and our intentions are clear. This takes honest effort and courage on our part.

- *How clearly do you express your intentions to each other?*
- *What responses from your partner provide you the most encouragement and support?*

Growth takes place one day at a time.

Be Creative Expressing Love

Our love, if it is to be genuine, must have the element of disquiet. This does not mean the disquiet that occurs when there is turmoil, doubt, or jealousy. It means that there is no constancy in which everything goes smoothly and without a hitch. It means that there is room for inventiveness in our relationships. Our life cannot always be predictable. If it is, sameness can set in and this is a close neighbor to boredom.

How inventive can you be in expressing your love to each other? For some of us this is a difficult task, but well worth the effort. Consider the different ways you express your loving and your caring to and for each other. Experience the similarities as well as the difference in your approach. Be patient and listen carefully to each other on this one.

* *What brings you the most pleasure and satisfaction in your relationship?*
* *How can you prevent boredom and sameness from taking over?*

Growth takes place one day at a time.

Complaining Again

Among some of the intentions behind complaining is "feeling free to speak out." This often takes some courage along with a healthy trust that it is truly justified and appropriate.

There are a number of biblical references, beginning with Moses claiming that God made a poor choice in choosing him for the job, to Jesus questioning his Father's will that he die on the cross. None of these suggest cowardice or unjustified complaints. They are, like so many others in the scripture, straightforward expressions of fear, uncertainty, anger, distrust, hope, and a lot of faith. Faith that it is okay to believe that God is big enough to handle our complaints because He understands the twists and turns of the human heart. We, of course, are not so gifted and have to struggle to understand not only the complaint but even more so, the complainer.

- *What complaints do you hear most often from each other?*
- *How are complaints dealt with in your relationship?*

Growth takes place one day at a time.

Awareness Of Your Feelings

Our feelings are a barometer of where we are at a given point in our day. There are many feelings that come and go. Some we are aware of more than others. We may or may not even be aware that there is no morality attached to our feelings. They are not accidental occurrences and, in fact, they always are the result of what is happening to us in our thoughts. We may not be in touch with our thoughts and we may be more aware of what we are feeling at a given moment.

With practice, we can sharpen our awareness of what we are saying to ourselves about a given situation and this awareness opens us up to the all important inner dialogue that goes on constantly within us. Listen for this inner dialogue as you deepen your awareness of your feelings. This can help you connect with your feelings and your partner.

- *How can your feelings serve as a barometer
in your relationship?*
- *What are some ways you can encourage the expression
of feelings with each other?*

Growth takes place one day at a time.

We Are All Earthen Vessels

The Apostle Paul in his second letter to the people of Corinth reminds us of our dignity as well as our weakness. As earthen vessels we are often troubled but not crushed, sometimes in doubt but never in despair; there are many enemies but we are never without a friend; and though badly hurt at times, we are never destroyed.

We are often reminded that we are strong and that we can handle anything that comes our way. We are in control of our own destiny. The other side of us is also true and that is the flip side of the coin. We are earthen vessels. We can feel strong and we can feel weak. It is never an either or. We should be able to experience the ups and downs of life and recognize that we have limitations. Yes, we are capable of exercising great courage and strength because we realize we also need others when we feel weak and fragile.

- *How safe do you feel with each other?*
- *What could you each do to promote more openness and less control of your true feelings in your relationship?*

Growth takes place one day at a time.

A Time Of Questioning

Do you ever find yourself thinking and wishing for the "good old days?" To have it as it once was. The security of knowing that you got through it all and that must count for something. Maybe it was your work, in the early struggles of your marriage; it could be that you just feel like you ran out of gas and your enthusiasm for new adventures or even new projects isn't the same as it once was. It becomes harder to get excited about things and you wonder about the cycles of your life and even your marriage.

This, of course, is not the time to panic nor even the time to be discouraged though God knows there are those moments. Today, we remind ourselves of what it takes to grow as a person and as a couple. Unless the seed dies (daily) it cannot spring into new life. This is a continuing process for us.

- *How do the words "unless the seeds dies it cannot spring to life" apply to your marriage?*
- *What happens when you have more questions than answers for the events in your life and marriage?*

Growth takes place one day at a time.

Time For Review

It is quite common for people in business to review goals and accomplishments. In your marriage, it can be useful also to review your goals. They may be long-term such as when to retire, what to do after retirement, how to raise children, etc... There may be personal goals you brought into the marriage that you may want your partner to know about and support.

Are these goals ever brought up and talked about? Is there a mutual agreement so that you experience a team effort and are moving in the same direction? There may be short-range goals relating to where you want to live and work. You may also discover that there are no goals that you have ever really discussed. This could be a good time to raise the subject of goals in your marriage and discuss what importance, if any, they have for you.

* *What are some of the personal and marriage goals*
up for review at this time?

Growth takes place one day at a time.

Being Present To Each Other

We all need our space to think our thoughts and feel what we feel. We also need to make the time for this to happen. Finding the time suggests that we know where to look.

Patience is required to be present for the other in our life, in our day. There will always be a certain amount of uncertainty, confusion, and risk in doing this. Being present to another is a powerful way of caring for that person. It allows for that other to be herself/himself in our presence. It is more than simply waiting passively for something to happen between us. It is respecting the timetable of the other. It is coming to believe that the other can grow and do so at his/her own pace. There is also the patience we must have with ourselves in giving ourselves permission to learn from the other and to discover ourselves in the process. Be patient in your efforts to care for each other.

- *How do you like your partner to be present for you?*
- *What could you learn from practicing being present*
  to each other?

Growth takes place one day at a time.

Being True To Yourself

Honesty has to do with integrity. It is more than not telling a lie. It has to do with genuine openness to ourselves and others. It means we are not necessarily going to be right. We attempt to see what really is and not only what we would like it to be. We cannot be interested only in being correct. We can be interested in pursuing where our awareness may tell us we are and even where we may need to go.

When integrity and honesty are actively present for us, we "ring true." Others come to trust and believe in us. There is no gap between what we say and what we do. We become less interested in how we come across because we now believe in ourselves. This allows us to be truly present for each other. Our love and caring comes alive. We are open to further growth.

- *How does being true to yourself make it possible to be more true to each other?*
- *What are some obstacles to maintaining integrity in your relationship?*

Growth takes place one day at a time.

Help Strengthen Each Other

Life can be burdensome. Your work may not be going well. You may be feeling the weight of your commitments to others. Whatever the situation you find yourself in today, you may hear the words of the old song, "Life gets tedious, don't it." Perhaps you recognize the wonderful intentions with which you began your marriage. With the passing of time and the many events that you experienced, you note how those ideals have gone through a lot of testing. Your faith in God may be the strength that is pulling you through the tight spots. The burden may not necessarily be getting lighter, but you feel the strength to at least manage it, carry it just a bit longer. You will get through it somehow. When you stumble, you get up and try again. You work together and your love is intact, refreshing though not inebriating. The burden is still here but so is the strength to carry it together. Share encouraging words and feelings with each other. Help lift each other up.

•What are some of the ways you lift each other up?
• How could this become a regular activity with each other?

Growth takes place one day at a time.

Giving The Gift Of Ourselves

Loving is giving without counting the cost. It is caring and sharing. It is being able to extend ourselves when we may feel we either have no more to give, or we simply don't feel like it. It is being able to pay attention and listen while bracketing our own needs at the time. The accent here is on our ability to give, not only of what we have materially, but mainly of ourselves. Our intentions are usually noble and sincere when we first marry. The edge on our generosity slowly wears down unless we maintain our vision of ourselves as gift bearers to each other.

- *Does giving of yourself seem difficult or somewhat natural and spontaneous?*
- *What is the greatest obstacle for you when it comes to giving of yourself?*
- *Are there certain circumstances, moods, feelings, attitudes, responses by your partner that come into play?*
- *Do you really believe that it is better to give than to receive?*

Growth takes place one day at a time.

Balancing Our Commitments

"We hardly see each other now. My work is getting me down, and there is so much of it. We just don't have time for each other anymore." If this sounds familiar, we may be considering our commitments and how they fit with the commitment we have to our marriage. Sometimes, we may recognize that some things simply have to go. We may realize that our marriage is out of balance. We are tiring in trying to keep everything afloat. When we try to eliminate this program, that activity, this project, we may feel guilty, angry and frustrated. We are left with the need to prioritize our time, intentions and our tasks as we consider just what toll it is all taking on our marriage.

- *Are you clear about quality and quantity time for and with each other?*
- *Look at your schedule for a week—personal, joint and family. Where does your marriage fit? How much time and attention is it getting?*

Growth takes place one day at a time.

When We Lack Control

One of the most difficult situations we can face is the one we have no control over. It may be a diagnosed illness or a circumstance we believe is out of our control. It may truly fit the part of the prayer that the alcoholic learns to pray, "to accept the things I cannot change." This truly is wisdom but so hard at times to put into practice. In fact, we tend to become anxious and stress-filled. We are unable to see how the situation can ever be remedied or the problem solved.

It is at these times that we may want to run away and hide or go to sleep hoping that when we awaken it will all be gone. It can be the time for sincere prayer. We ask for courage to face it with a deep faith and the willingness to learn how to manage the problem. To stay with it until we figure out what to do next. This takes courage. Support from each other can be very meaningful and helpful at this time.

- *Is there any situation in your life or in your relationship over which you feel you have no control?*
- *How are you attempting to deal with it?*
- *What support do you receive from each other?*

Growth takes place one day at a time.

Managing For Awhile

Today may be one of those days when we need to hear the words, "take courage, hang in there, I am here for you." This may be the time when our spirits are low and we are not at our best. We come to realize that we can have highs and lows, ups and downs. Yesterday may even have been a high–but today is something different. We fight the battle today. We need to go on even though we want to languish, hang around, and even dwell on the negative side of things.

Is there any joy in all of this? Can our spirits be lifted? What about a walk, a change of scenery, a movie, a phone call, something to take us out of the doldrums? It will pass, it usually does. We will find a way–we usually do. We may need to reach out again. We may need a helping hand, or to hear the words, "I am here for you."

• Are there times in your life, and perhaps in your marriage, when you feel you are barely hanging on? What are those times?
• Do you feel and believe that your partner is really there for you when you need him/her?

Growth takes place one day at a time.

Love Without Conditions

We may be more familiar with loving than with being loved. Recognizing a lack of love in our lives can be painful. We may recall how love was not available to us at earlier stages in our lives. Such a deficit of love can often leave us with a sense of emptiness. We attempt to fill the void with various means such as feverish activities, drugs, and alcohol. It is important that we acknowledge that need for love and personal value.

We need to be with those who affirm us and who love us unconditionally. There must be no condition, no strings attached. We have a God who loves us unconditionally, no strings attached. He was first to love us and that will never change. You are fortunate if you have a partner who loves you and is a prescription of love for you. Give thanks and be grateful, for you are truly blessed.

> • *Are you feeling loved unconditionally?*
> • *How does your partner contribute to this love?*
> • *How are both of you striving for this kind of love in your relationship?*

Growth takes place one day at a time.

Honesty In Your Convictions

How honest can we be with ourselves? We can bring joy to another, but we alone can give integrity to ourselves. Do you hide your convictions about certain things in your life? Are there certain areas in your life that you know and believe you will certainly stand up for? Are you really sure? Have you been really tested? Do you ever look to your partner to rescue you and take you off the hook? Are you allowing your partner to speak for you and thus allowing yourself to continue along the safe path, the path of least resistance?

Few of us will ever be asked to compromise our life over a situation or event. However, we may be faced with the possibility of compromising a principle or a value that we thought was intact.

* *How do you stand up for what you truly believe?*
* *Does your partner know what your convictions really are?*

Growth takes place one day at a time.

Let Yourself Wonder

Let's just make this a "wonder day." Turn off the light, close your eyes, stop talking for a moment, and just wonder. Wonder about who you are–what makes you so unique–where are you headed if you keep going in your present direction–what would you be doing if you weren't doing what you are right now? These are just suggestions to open yourself up to the wonder of wondering. This gets you in touch with that active little child within you who can become most creative if allowed to be.

If you have difficulty getting into this exercise, it can be helpful to just go along with whatever permissions you can give yourself to wonder, and simply daydream. By the way, the latter was usually strictly forbidden and looked down upon at one time. Remember? No more restrictions. Let go. It's O.K. Do this in a safe place.

• How safe is it for you to let yourself daydream?
• How safe is it to share your fantasies, your daydreams,
your wonderings with your partner?

Growth takes place one day at a time.

Compatibility–The Myth

Compatibility is one of those "loaded" words that at first glance is something you look for in a successful and happy marriage. As you look further, however, it takes on the look of a not so attractive picture. Like equality, it has its problems. If we all thought alike, felt alike and acted alike, what a boring world and marriage we would have.

At one time, in the past, our culture, legal system, and even our churches supported security and predictability at all costs. Very few were asking if we were satisfied and happy. The main thing was to place our noses to the grindstone, buck up like little campers and offer it up. Today we can deal with our incompatibility. Both can see things differently, and it can become a spice for life. Of course, it takes practice, good communication skills and a whole lot of goodwill, but it is all worth the effort.

- *What does compatibility mean to you?*
- *How important is it for your relationship?*

Growth takes place one day at a time.

Recognizing Our Limitations

How often have you heard or even said yourself, "I've lost it," "I don't have it anymore." The implication is that we have become aware of some capacity that is no longer functioning as it once did. The admission to myself or another may merely signal the natural movement from one phase of my life to another. In this case, it is quite natural, but we can become discouraged and frightened. Such discoveries about ourselves can be helpful and beneficial when we are able to share them with another. As we advance in age, we pray for the advancement in wisdom as well.

We need to recognize that we enter a holding pattern after the second decade of our lives. This pattern leads to a physical down-spiral, and should prompt us to deepen our awareness and share our personal discoveries with each other. These can be special moments as we move along in our marriage journey.

- *How can the recognition and admission of your personal limitations help your relationship?*
- *What limitations in your marriage can you share openly with each other?*

Growth takes place one day at a time.

Testing Our Love

Our love for each other is being tested and tried daily. Often, we are not even aware of it. A situation or circumstance can offer an opportunity to consider the security and happiness of the other person in our life. It is difficult to consider their needs immediately because such a frame of reference is not common for most of us. We walk into most situations carrying our own agenda, our own needs, wishes and wants.

True loving takes a lot of hard work, doesn't it? Many of us fair poorly. The old driving force is what we refer to as "romance" is no longer as strong, or personal. This is when we may panic or at least experience disillusion at its worst. Can you identify with these challenges to your love for each other? Perhaps a little review would be helpful.

- *How is your love for each other being tested right now?*
- *How are you personally dealing with this? Are you involving your partner?*

Growth takes place one day at a time.

Honoring The Child Within

While outside running this morning, I thought of the words in James Cavanaugh's poem, "Little boy, where are you?" I began to cry. I thought back on my own life as I felt the tears on my cheek. I could recall incidents and happenings that told me how aware I was of the little things. I wondered, when did I close my eyes, turn off my curiosity and freeze my emotions?

Where is your little boy? Where is your little girl? Can you take another look today? Perhaps you will find him or her. They are not far away. You may have just lost touch. You may notice this in the way you worry, the way you plan, the way you feel. Today is a reminder of how much we need to treasure our present moments. Look around and see what you see. Take it in and relish it. It is all you have right now. You are precious. Treasure your specialness.

• Little child where are you?
*• How can you nurture the child within yourself
and in your partner?*

Growth takes place one day at a time.

Make Your Love Known

When was the last time you told others in your presence that you loved your partner? So often we tell others how well he or she does with the kids. We say he or she is putting in a lot of hours. Are we embarrassed or afraid of something? Do we possibly hide behind the secretive view of our relationship and simply consider it all too private to express in public? Maybe this has an influence as to why we stop holding hands, opening car doors, and all those little things we "used to do."

Perhaps a little more openness and risk-taking in these little things could send a powerful message that we are all in this together. We can learn from each other, and especially from those little expressions of tenderness.

• *How do you make your love for each other known to others?*
• *Why is it important to keep your marriage relationship a private affair?*

Growth takes place one day at a time.

Our Bias May Be Showing

Our questions often say more about our beliefs underlying the questions, than the impact of the questions themselves. Our own male or female biases do come out in different ways "Why are so few top positions held by women?" "Why are men so preoccupied with themselves, while women seem to share so easily?" Do we ever experience ourselves stressing the differences to possibly feed our own biases?

We often smile at the references we read or hear about. Our awareness of our own beliefs about the differences between us can help us question some of our own long-held beliefs and stereotypes. Even our churches are becoming more aware of how they have fostered and supported old beliefs and myths, and today they are being seriously challenged. Take time to share your views with each other, and especially in the area of the roles you have assumed in your relationship.

- *How does gender bias show up in your marriage?*
- *What are the stereotypes and myths in your relationship?*

Growth takes place one day at a time.

Our Feeling Of Rejection

Is there anyone you know who has not felt rejection? I doubt it. What is this feeling? Is it a kind of sadness, disappointment, anger, all of the above? What brings it on? On closer examination, we may notice that it has a connection with what we think and believe about a given situation. When we are more aware of our own thoughts and intentions, we may become somewhat surprised that the feeling is of our own making. It is what we tell ourselves about what is happening to us that triggers the accompanying feelings.

This should not make us unwilling to reach out and risk disapproval or fail to stand up for what we believe. Besides, our risk can be a seed of encouragement for someone who may be less assertive, easily hurt, scared, and prone to giving up easily. Take a closer look at the feelings of rejection and allow that look to help you grow as a person and as a couple.

- *In what situations do you feel most rejected in your relationship?*
- *How could your partner help you discover the thoughts and feelings underlying your feelings of rejection?*

Growth takes place one day at a time.

Our Children

Today, if you have children, consider your relationship with them, whether they are with you or have already left the home. How would you describe your relationship with each child? Would you say you are close and there is a mutual understanding and acceptance? What is it that you most want for your children? Do these wants reflect your own personal goals and values? Do you really believe in them and their unique potential to be successful and happy human beings? Do you consider them to already be "whole and complete" or do you perceive them still "on the way to becoming whole and unique?" Do you praise them frequently and look for something to praise rather than find fault?

Our children are on loan to us. We never owned them. Let's pray for them and for ourselves. We want to appreciate ourselves and them as gifts to each other. Share your appreciation and well wishes with them when you can.

- *How do your wants for your children reflect your own personal goals, wants and desires?*
- *What can your children teach you about parenting and unconditional love?*

Growth takes place one day at a time.

Respect Your Loneliness

When we feel alone, even in a group, we can usually find someone to be with and that seems to take care of the matter. It is more difficult when we experience loneliness. Often, we sense something deeper and personal. We may recognize a strong desire to reach out to another, but there is a realization that something is missing. We may believe we don't have the tools to do that. There may be a recognition of shyness and even an awkwardness in our efforts to relate.

Perhaps, we believed that marrying would take care of it somehow and make it all better. We now face the task of learning new skills, gaining confidence in our ability to build bridges to another. This can seem hard and uncomfortable, but we can try. We can also ask our partner to help us.

- *What are the times when you feel most lonely?*
- *What is it that you most need at that time?*
- *How would you like your partner to be present for you?*

Growth takes place one day at a time.

Acknowledging Our Differences

Many of us have been raised to be courteous and considerate of the needs of others. It is important to use tact and diplomacy. There are benefits that come from delaying our own gratification. Many of us try to practice this in our marriage and consider any break in the cooperative system to surely mean our marriage is in trouble.

The truth of the matter is that we are different from one another. Different interests, needs, and wants are a healthy sign and need to be treated as such. When we can obtain the agreement of another and even match desires, intentions, and needs, it can be very beneficial and rewarding. Most often, this is difficult to accomplish, and to strain for such compatibility at the expense of being honest with our own legitimate needs and wants may be counterproductive. A look at how this could apply may be helpful. Let's appreciate what we have.

- *What are the main differences in your relationship?*
- *How are these differences respected and dealt with?*
- *How can your differences be used positively in your marriage?*

Growth takes place one day at a time.

What A Comforting Thought

We often seek support and encouragement from others. This is fine and necessary. Today, however, let's think a comforting thought. What is that for us?

Perhaps we are in the midst of making an important decision or we may be down or frustrated over something in our life. On the other hand, this day may be just terrific and we may be filled with all kinds of positive self-messages. Whatever your situation is today, look for a comforting thought for yourself. Let it be uplifting and let it show you its comforting embrace. Perhaps you can bring this comforting thought to mind at different times of your day and then take it to rest with you for the night. Share it with your partner if you like.

- *What comforting thought can you give yourself today?*
- *What comforting words can you give to your partner today?*

Growth takes place one day at a time.

The Gift Of Time

"I don't have time," "I can't find time," "There is no time," "Time waits for no one," and so on. We have heard most of these references and no doubt have used them ourselves. It is a sober thought that the clock is our structure for measuring our daily activity.

"Now is the acceptable time–this is the day of our salvation," says Paul in the letter to the Corinthians. Each day is a gift. What are you doing with this special gift? This day is ours to live. These are our moments never again to be experienced. For some, one day is the same as the next or a carbon copy of the previous day. What if we were to live each day as if it were our last? Would anything change? Would we change the way we live–the way we spend our time–the priorities we have? What other areas of our lives would be affected if we lived each day to the fullest–each day as if it were our last?

- *What does time hold out to you?*
- *How can this day be a gift for you and each other?*

Growth takes place one day at a time.

Saying You Are Sorry

For some of us, saying "I'm sorry," is very difficult. We may never even think of it and it becomes left out of our vocabulary. I recently witnessed two people wounding each other with their harsh comments and their defensive words. Neither was able to obtain "victory," and each was spilling out their underlying hurt and pain in protective ways. Saying "I'm sorry" could not even enter into their minds and hearts as they saw each other as enemies and threats to their own security and safety.

Love and hate are four letter words, but that is where the similarity ends. Often there is a very fine line between the two. We are all capable of expressing both.

- *Consider any scenes in your life in which one or the other may be occurring, perhaps with some regularity.*
- *See if you can identify any examples of either in your own life or in the lives of others around you.*

Growth takes place one day at a time.

Serendipity

Surprises can be "huge fun." What child isn't always in the mood for a happy surprise or two. They are usually easily given and easily received. Going with the flow is easy.

As we get older, they can also be "huge fun." They can require additional safeguards to pull them off. One of the necessary ingredients is to make certain that it does not turn out to be a dud. A wonderful intention to surprise your partner with a special dinner without an advance check of the schedule could turn a loving gesture into a very troubling evening. A straightforward invitation can often do wonders. Checking in with each other by phone can be a simple way to handle last minute changes. How about cooking up a surprise?

• How are surprises given and received in your relationship?
• How can you make surprises an important ingredient
in your marriage?

Growth takes place one day at a time.

The Wedding Is Not The Marriage

It does not take very long after marrying to realize that our wedding is not our marriage. Just a short time before, we were single, on our own, and now in a short time we are expected to grow up, be an adult, a terrific problem solver, lover, and effective communicator. In short, somehow we are to possess all that it takes to make our marriage successful and happy.

Whatever fantasies we have or had about marriage now continue to be challenged and slowly abandoned. Our perspective should now be closer to reality. It takes time and great effort to build a successful relationship. It does not just happen accidentally. All of us have been given the bare, raw talents.

- *How are you using yours?*
- *What are you building?*
- *What is your marriage like right now?*
- *What do you want it to become?*

Growth takes place one day at a time.

Complaining Again!

We need positive, clear and constructive ways to express our thoughts and feelings. It is a real blessing to ourselves and others when we can express our dissatisfactions, disappointments and frustrations, clearly and without blame. One helpful way is to attach your request to your complaint. This informs your partner of an underlying need or want that often goes unnoticed in the heat of the complaint or frustration.

When we leave out our request and go only with the complaint or frustration our partner hears only half of the story. Strange as it may seem, our complaints can be constructive vehicles to express what is happening for us at a particular time. We can learn to complain with a purpose. There may be old mental prescriptions like "keep it to yourself," "no one really cares," "be satisfied with what you have," "offer it up, it will go away."

> • *How are complaints expressed and received*
> *in your relationship?*
> • *Do your complaints also contain a verbal request?*
> • *How can you make your complaints positive vehicles for your*
> *needs and wants?*

Growth takes place one day at a time.

Consistency Builds Trust

Trusting is one of the qualities we gain for ourselves at an early age. This quality is not purely personal nor is it static. The promises we make at the time of our marriage, such as love, cherish, trust, are involved in an ongoing process. We need to establish consistency in our behavior. It is when our actions match our intentions that we experience ourselves trusting and being trusted.

Trust can only be developed over a long period of time. It occurs because of the consistency that we experience with each other. As we live together, we continue to form consistent ways of talking and listening to each other. We do not have to read between the lines because we are reading each other clearly. If doubt occurs or communication becomes muddled, we can feel free to clarify the situation immediately.

• Are you building trust with each other?
• Are there areas of consistency in your life and relationship?

Growth takes place one day at a time.

Putting Our Maps Together

Each of us, growing up, designed our own map for reality. We added and deleted as we moved along on our journey. When we marry, we bring the map of life and reality with us. Since it is familiar to us, and us alone, we rely upon it to get us through life. As we bring it to our marriage, we must be ready again to add and delete, change a direction, and add a stop. These are adjustments we must make and it can become difficult and frustrating at times. We need to have a lot of courage and the desire to learn and unlearn. The latter is often the most difficult because we tend to hang on to the familiar, even when we are aware that it is not working. To be open to learning about your own map and the map of your partner can be a very positive and enriching goal for your relationship.

- *How clear is the map you brought with you to your marriage?*
- *How can you help learn about each other's map? And each other?*

Growth takes place one day at a time.

Give Yourself Some Time

Ecclesiastes speaks of a time for everything that happens to us. It suggests that we know when to begin and when to stop. It is wisdom to know when to move on. There is such a wisdom in the serenity prayer. "God grant me the serenity to accept the things I cannot change, the courage to change the things I can, and the wisdom to know the difference."

There are old feelings that may need to be placed in a new perspective. There are tasks that need to be abandoned because the reasons for doing them have changed. There are decisions requiring a fresh assessment. There are old hurts that have turned into long and unnecessary suffering. For the sake of personal peace and enrichment of yourself and your marriage, you may need to move off and move on. Identifying exactly when and how to do this requires personal prayer, discernment, and courage. Today is a good time to begin.

- *How can you be more patient with the changes occurring in your relationship?*
- *How can you best use your time to help you and your relationship?*

Growth takes place one day at a time.

Relief Is Spelled–JOY

Are you experiencing relief or are you experiencing joy? We know there must be suffering, pain, and disappointment in our lives. When we pass through these times, it is possible that joy can enter or we can merely be relieved.

What is your attitude today? Do you have a vision for tomorrow? Are you hopeful? Are you down and gloomy about what your day is today? What is needed for you to turn things around? What needs to be changed? Is it your attitude, your vision, your inner conversation with yourself? Can you accept your pain, your disappointment and take it for what it is so you can learn from it? This could place you in a good position for experiencing joy instead of gloom. The choice is yours. Consider the balance of joy and pain in your life and marriage.

- *In what areas of your marriage are you seeking relief?*
- *How can you help bring relief and joy to those areas?*

Growth takes place one day at a time.

Express Your Needs Openly

"Everybody needs somebody sometimes." These are words of a song and they are reasonable and true. We all need others in our lives at different times and for different needs. This does not mean that we are dependent upon them for our self-worth. We can and need to keep our self worth intact. This is something we give to ourselves.

Do you ever act as if you really do not need anyone? You may even foster the impression that you are sufficient unto yourself. This can be dangerous and could contribute to isolation, separation, and disconnectedness. You may perceive yourself as weak and lacking backbone when you express your needs openly to another. It seems as though God himself needs us to make things work here on earth. He does not directly intervene in life's events ordinarily. Take this as a cue to accept your own neediness. We need God and we need each other. We need love, encouragement, support in our journey in life. As a couple, we need to express our needs openly and honestly.

- *When do you most need your partner?*
- *How do you currently respond to each other's needs?*

Growth takes place one day at a time.

The Signs In Our Life

Some things sneak up on us—or do they? Are things there all the while and is it that we just do not notice them? They are like those little reflectors along the curve in the road that we ordinarily only notice at night. They are true guides to that turn in the road. There are some guides along our journey in life that are present and that we hardly notice. They may be internal such as headaches, tiredness, and pain. They may be external, such as a comment by a friend, an unexpected incident, or an event that occurs with some frequency.

Reflect on some of the guideposts along your way. Share these with your partner. They may reveal some new and helpful insights to learn from.

- *What are some of the internal and external signs in your life right now?*
- *What could they be pointing to that could be helpful to you and your relationship?*

Growth takes place one day at a time.

Principles And Peace

All of us want peace, in the world around us and in our own inner world. We know this is not easily achieved on either level. Emerson once wrote, "Nothing can bring you peace but yourself; nothing can bring you peace but the triumph of principles."

Living your life based on principles is an honorable goal. It takes courage and persistent effort. First of all, you need to identify these principles for yourself. You can easily react to people and situations with a quickness that can trigger your reactions and not evaluate them in the light of your principles for life. What causes you to experience inner peace for yourself, your marriage, your home? You cannot bring peace to others unless you possess it yourself.

• Are you at peace today?
•What principles in your life contribute to you being at peace with yourself and others?

Growth takes place one day at a time.

Being Free To Learn

One cannot seriously study or discuss freedom and not consider the life and teaching of Jesus. He challenged any teaching, religious or civil, that threatened or minimized the dignity of life. He was confronted by the religious of his day because he favored bending, and even dismissing, a law when its application violated sensitivity to natural and human need. They would look at the law and he would look always to the heart. In each instance, he would go deeper.

When his accusers finally killed him, they would not even allow themselves to face the real issues with which Jesus was dealing. They chose, rather, to boil it all down to Jesus being a political revolutionary. They were blind to the very end. Their rigid adherence to their views never changed. Is there anything we can learn from this?

• How rigidly do you hang on to your views?
• How open are you to learning from each other?

Growth takes place one day at a time.

Touching The Ordinary

There are experiences we have that amaze us. It may be a new discovery or opportunity, a trip or spectacular view. We experience ourselves exhilarated and even awed. While these are powerful and influential, it is still the ordinary stuff that challenges us daily and demands meaning and direction. The commonplace, ordinary, no frills routine of our day is what we deal with.

Along with these ordinary events and circumstances come opportunities to offer powerful gestures of concern, love, and caring to others in our life. There is the time we take to say hello, the hand on the shoulder of a depressed friend, the hug for our partner, or the pat on the back encouraging a child to keep up the effort. These are the opportunities, the gestures, the caring responses to those ordinary human occurrences we face each day.

- *What is your attitude toward the ordinariness in your life?*
- *How does this attitude affect the way you live your life?*
- *What implications does this have for your marriage?*

Growth takes place one day at a time.

Moving From Heat To Light

Where there is heat, there is fire. When we have a fight there are a lot of feelings expressed, but the source is not always known. The light or insight comes when we understand and learn from the fight or argument. This seldom, if ever, occurs at the time of the disagreement. Our involvement at the moment is getting all of our attention. The heat is turned on.

Our first clue as to how deep our feelings run and how quickly they are triggered is when we recognize that they got turned on without our awareness and over our good intentions. This is because what is happening is in some way out of our awareness. We can repeat the argument over and over. Hence, there is a lot of heat, and not much light. Recognition of what is happening takes time and effort to learn.

- *What issues trigger the strongest emotional reactions from you and your partner?*
- *What are you learning about yourself and your relationship from these reactions?*

Growth takes place one day at a time.

A Wasted Energy

Our worries are driven by fear-the fear that is fueled by catastrophic beliefs. Only about eight percent are tied to realities that exist. Therefore, a high percentage are rooted in expectations of the worst that could happen to us. Usually these fearful expectations involve a barrage of "what if's." What if this or that happened? There is a major difficulty separating possibilities from probabilities.

There need to be specific answers given to "what if's" in order for worry to lose its grip on us. When we answer specifically we can sort out our beliefs and the solutions begin to replace our misdirected fears. An anonymous writer once wrote, "Don't tell me that worry doesn't do any good. I know better. The things I worry about don't happen." Worry is believed to be a form of control over the bad things we expect to happen to us.

•How much does worry affect your personal life and your relationship?

• What can you do to reduce the unnecessary worry in your life?

• How could your partner be of help to you in this?

Growth takes place one day at a time.

What's It All About?

We are all busy finding and giving meaning to the various events in our lives. This is our task and our responsibility as adults. When we do not experience meaning, we search for substitutes and alternatives. It is at this time that we look for some kind of anchor. We seek someone or something to distract us from our hollow feelings and our loneliness. The discovery of living without such an anchor, without meaning for the many events and activities in our lives, can leave us desperate and confused.

This is our opportunity to reach deeper. To look more deeply into the secrets of life itself. Why am I here? Where am I going? Is there something beyond my present life and circumstances? It is important that you share these questions, these moments with your partner.

- *What provides you with meaning for your life?*
- *How could your answer affect your relationship with each other?*

Growth takes place one day at a time.

The Choices We Are Making

Our life is often uneventful. There is a certain predictability to our life. The experience of making choices may seem limited to the mundane and ordinary. There come times when the need to make choices does present itself. This may not only involve a choice between good and bad, but a choice between two goods. Sometimes our choices seem to benefit us in one way and may be detrimental and harmful in another way. Some of our choices may be good for the short term and destructive for the long term.

Being able to discern the benefits and the disadvantages requires prayerful discernment. We may need to assess our basic stance. Are you living a totally reactive lifestyle and avoiding experiencing yourself directing your life responsibly? What is your basic stance in life?

- *What value do you personally place in making choices for yourself?*
- *Do you share your choices and decisions with each other?*

Growth takes place one day at a time.

Valuing Our Freedom

Freedom means different things to different people. We may be curtailed and confined, yet experience a true freedom inside. The truth here is that we do not take our freedom lightly. We do not give it away nor do we allow anyone to take it from us.

There are numerous lessons in history where, during confinement, internal freedom was never lost. This was often the case during war atrocities. The freedom within us can only be threatened from inside. When we lose our internal freedom, we become slaves to our compulsions, addictions, and our ego. To be creative, we must be free inside. An honest and open discussion with your partner could be profitable and helpful.

- *What obstacles do you experience that hinder your creativity in your life and in your marriage?*
- *How could the experience of personal inner freedom help your marriage?*

Growth takes place one day at a time.

Check Out Our Realities

Whose reality is it-ours or someone else's? We often do not see reality the same as others. When this occurs, especially in our relationships, it may call for some concern. We all have a picture in our own mind as to how reality should exist. This can cause us to see reality not as it really is, but rather how we expect it to be. In fact, we may come on strong with others simply to enforce our own perceptions.

We all need to have a way of assessing our realities, at least the way we perceive them. One way is to promote learning something by checking things out with each other. This can be helpful and it indicates a sense of fairness and an eagerness to be open to learning. We all have our own filters through which we see the world around us.

- *What are the times you feel far apart and distant from your partner?*
- *How do you handle these times alone and with each other?*

Growth takes place one day at a time.

The Direction We Are Going

Having a direction for our life is related to our basic philosophy of how we give meaning to our life—the way we treat life, all of life, animate and inanimate. We place our life in jeopardy with our little compromises, our passivity, our failure to declare who we are and what we want our life to be.

Unrealistic dependency upon others and failure to declare our intentions openly leaves room for discounting ourselves and our values. Look at the direction you are currently giving to your life and decide who and what is influencing your direction. Who is at the helm? How clear is your vision of where you are going? Are where you are and what you currently are doing going to get you there?

* *In what direction do you envision yourself personally going at this time in your life?*
* *In what direction do you envision your marriage going?*
* *How is your personal vision connected to the vision of your marriage?*

Growth takes place one day at a time.

Always Communicating

There is no such thing as not communicating. From time to time, it is important to check out this reality in our relationships. Our words, gestures, sounds, intonations, silences, and moods all say something to others about ourselves. These may or may not exactly say what we want to say. There is no guarantee that we will not be misunderstood. We usually play our part, however, in the misunderstanding. We can then easily feel irritated and anxious with the other person.

It is important that we be as clear as possible so as to avoid uttering those "cutesie" remarks or becoming very indirect and playing the twenty question game. These provide barriers to the much needed clear and direct communications vital for a mutually satisfying relationship. Check this one out with each other.

- *How do you feel about the way you express yourself?*
- *What can each of you do to make your communication with each other more clear, direct, and open?*

Growth takes place one day at a time.

Guiding Our Own Spirit

The human spirit is wonderfully complicated. Many of us have been brought up to believe that happiness has a terrible price tag. Or we may believe that striving for success and material possessions is our only way to happiness. Few have been more successful than Marilyn Monroe or Judy Garland-so much success and limelight and yet so much unhappiness and misfortune.

Can you identify with values that limit you to fleeting pleasures and short-sightedness? Does your own human spirit reach for what is more durable and lasting to the human heart? This can provide some assurance that only we can truly restrain our human spirit. Conformity to someone else's values and standards can be too high a price for us to follow.

- *What are some of your strong values guiding your life right now?*
- *What significance do these values have for your marriage?*

Growth takes place one day at a time.

Those Early Years

The process of adjustment, especially early in marriage, is difficult and often tedious. There can exist a conflict between intimacy and the need for independence. We may become uncertain of how much we can give of ourselves without losing ourselves in the process. It may come as a shock to us that we can not be everything to our partner. This is a natural and healthy reality in every marriage. It is a necessary separation, though it may be difficult to accept.

With time and much effort to understand, we can work toward balance. We can recognize and learn to appreciate our partner's unique personality and accept his or her uniqueness and individuality as a separateness that is an essential part of our love for each other. When we lose one argument, we do not lose them all. When we have one fight, we do not always fight.

• How do you experience your separateness in your marriage?
• What value, if any, can the experience of separateness
have for your relationship?

Growth takes place one day at a time.

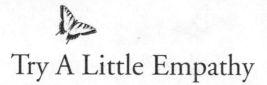

Try A Little Empathy

It may surprise us to learn that most of us are not very tolerant of the feelings of those around us. It is difficult not to expect others to see reality as we do, and feel the same feelings as we do. In our relationship, we can easily translate mutuality as, "If you love me, you will see and do it my way."

A way of combating this is to make a strong effort to understand the other's beliefs, feelings, and actions. Try to place ourselves in that other person's shoes. It is as if silently we are asking, "How does he or she feel?" "How would I feel if this were done to me?" "Why did they do what they did?" "What good reason did they have for doing it?" This is our effort to be empathetic with others in our life. This precludes the demand, "You must think, believe, feel, and act like me."

• *How do you experience empathy in your relationship?*
• *Why is it the essential ingredient in all successful communication?*

Growth takes place one day at a time.

There Is More Ahead

It was Alexander The Great who allegedly said, "There are no more worlds for me to conquer." He died believing he did it all. Consider how far we have come since then. There is no one of us who has done it all.

Who of us can say that there is not one more mountain to climb, one more challenge to face, one more struggle to overcome? Can we afford to stop trying to do a better job, have a happier marriage, make our home more peaceful, try one more time? Fear and a false sense of assurance can prevent us from reaching out and looking ahead. Complacency can deaden us in our tracks. We really are not finished with our task.

• Consider what more you have to do. What projects need completion?
•What aspect in your marriage could use some loving attention?

Growth takes place one day at a time.

Be Direct And Avoid Blaming

We can involve ourselves in a cold war when we resort to using the blaming game in our relationships. This isn't always so obvious to us. We can hide our blame behind sullen or guilt behavior, and not reveal our underlying hurt and anger. We can find ourselves waiting for the other to make a move while guardedly holding ourselves back for fear of anticipated rejection.

Much of our blame can be related to our failure to make known our thoughts, feelings, and wants at a particular time. The delay in expressing ourselves directly can cause something to fester in us and come out in some form of guerrilla warfare. Setting up a process by which we are determined to negotiate our wants and express ourselves directly can short-circuit any blaming game.

> • *How direct can you be in expressing your thoughts and feelings to your partner?*
> • *What is needed for this to happen in your relationship?*

Growth takes place one day at a time.

Risk Taking The First Step

Someone recently said to me, "I want to avoid being indifferent." It scared her to think she could protect herself by becoming indifferent to her partner. She could hide behind her work, her books, and not let him get to her. This enabled her to avoid her real fear by making him unimportant and thus unable to hurt her.

We all have our ways of protecting ourselves. When indifference meets indifference, chances are there is a deep separation in the relationship. Needs are not being met and such a relationship could be in real trouble. Indifference needs confrontation. Waiting for the other to make the first move is very risky. Someone needs to risk taking the first step. Often it pays off with wonderful results.

- *Is there any area in your relationship in which you are waiting for your partner to take the initiative?*
- *What are some safeguards to indifference in your marriage?*

Growth takes place one day at a time.

Our Love Challenges Us

Love challenges us to get to our true selves. On one hand it asks the question, how much can we be ourselves and to what degree do we sacrifice ourselves for each other? It can ask, how much do we take the role of supporter and helper without expecting the same in return? It can challenge our independence in the relationship in terms of just how much autonomy or independence is needed. Love questions how much there needs to be a rhythm of strength and weakness without either person becoming fixed in one or the other.

We learn to listen to the challenge of our love along our journey together. We seek to discover and bring into life along the way the full force of our personalities and commitment. This can be truly challenging and lovingly rewarding.

- *How do you experience your love for your partner challenging you?*
- *Which of these challenges is the toughest to deal with right now?*

Growth takes place one day at a time.

Our Listening Skills Are Needed

The powerful and much needed skill of listening needs to be renewed from time to time. We need to reaffirm our decision to be sensitive and effective listeners. When we fail along the way, we can openly and honestly say to another, "I'm sorry. I just wasn't listening–will you repeat that again?" It is helpful to visualize ourselves as effective and caring listeners. We see ourselves in our mind's eye first and then do it in action.

Of course, it always helps to pat ourselves on the back and give ourselves praise for our efforts and our successes. This is a skill not achieved overnight. It takes perseverance, failures, little successes along the way, and practice, practice, practice. Reward yourself when you succeed and listen to positive feedback to the sincere efforts you are making.

• How well do you listen to your partner?
• How well does your partner listen to you?
• What effort are you making to become a more effective listener?

Growth takes place one day at a time.

Love Follows An Unsmooth Course

For many of us, life is more a problem to be solved than a life to be lived. Love takes on a quality and search for perfection instead of a simple experience to enjoy and relish. As we try to harness our love and even enshrine it, we fear we will lose it. We question its durability and longevity. We take precautions so as not to awaken one day and discover it gone. We get busy and active so we can preserve our love from decay or disappearance.

It is difficult to accept that our love rides the very rough waters we attempt to control or ignore. It grows and thrives amidst our graying hair, wrinkles, and accumulated emotional scars. Our love for each other is very human, and therefore grows slowly and unevenly. It surprises us and always challenges us with an unsteady rhythm. It defies our control and always welcomes our openness.

- *How has your love for each other pulled or pushed you through the rough times in your marriage?*
- *What are you doing to nurture and strengthen your love for each other?*

Growth takes place one day at a time.

Our Standard For Action

We act differently when we are alone and when we are with others. Is this because the standard we follow is different in each instance? If so, it would be well to consider scenes in which we know this to be true. Does human respect influence the way you live?

There are stories we could all tell in which we compromised ourselves in some way. Being a principled person takes courage, integrity, and a life rooted in values. Of course, we know there are ideals. We often do not want to pay the price this requires. Consider the standards you try to live by. Are these compromised by your mood or the respect and approval of others?

• Is there a noticeable difference in what you do privately and what you do together as a couple?
• Are you a person for all seasons but rooted in none?
• How true for you is the statement, "everyone has his/her price"?

Growth takes place one day at a time.

We Are Good Enough

It is difficult for some of us to accept ourselves as good persons. We screen all affirmations through narrow lenses. We become fearful and anxious with others in anticipation that they will spot our defects and surely see us as we really are. Our life becomes a steady flow of protections from others, ourselves, and even our God.

Facing the truth of who we are is a lifetime task. The true portrait of ourselves will hardly ever become known except for the constant observation of our God, who accepts us for what we truly are. If we see God as a rigid taskmaster who is preoccupied with our mistakes and failures, then we nurture an image of ourselves that supports a false and damaging judgment. It is difficult to face ourselves honestly and still accept and love ourselves as we really are. If we are good enough people for God, we are good enough for ourselves.

- *Do you believe that at your core, you are a good person? If so, why? If not, why not?*
- *How does having a strong positive self-image help in the way you see and experience your partner?*

Growth takes place one day at a time.

Our Family Ties

Our experiences often dictate our expectations. Our view of what a family "should be" is conditioned by our experience with our own family. Family ties are strong and weak depending on what we envision them being and becoming. We may feel the strain in establishing close relationships with members of our families. Our partner has his or her experiences that are important to understand. Appreciating our need for these close relationships can be challenging and tedious.

Our efforts provide a powerful source for appreciating our partner. Our history can supply a rich background for respecting each other's current beliefs, feelings, and behavior. The opportunities for close contact with family and relatives open doors to growing personally and as a couple. An active interest and involvement in each other's family can enlarge the circle of your close friends.

- *How close do you feel to each other's family and relatives?*
- *How could fostering friendships with each other's families help your own relationship?*

Growth takes place one day at a time.

Open To Intimacy

When we share with the intention of understanding ourselves and each other, we open the door to intimacy. This door is opened when we experience acceptance. There is a deep sense of respect for self and each other. Of course, this is not easy to come by.

We can come to easily tolerate each other's values, beliefs, behaviors, and feelings. When we sense this, the wall of separation goes up. To feel tolerated is to feel isolated and on guard. Accepting each other does not mean total agreement. It simply involves no judgments. Often, we can say we do not understand and mean it. This is a good beginning. The next step is to express a genuine and sincere intention to learn and understand. Most of us are willing to accept the sincere learner, especially if it is our partner. Sharing and exploring together can lead to acceptance, understanding and intimacy.

- *How does acceptance of each other lead to greater intimacy?*
- *What restrictions are currently preventing mutual understanding and acceptance in your relationship?*

Growth takes place one day at a time.

Connected To The Source

In poignant terms, Jeremiah of the Old Testament describes what happens when we remain connected to the Source, our God. We are as trees growing near a stream, sending our roots deep to a water supply. We are not bothered by bad weather or conditions on the surface because we are connected to the Source. It is because of this condition that we bear fruit. This is not our personal gift alone. We must not become complacent and oblivious to others around us. Our connection with the Source, vital as it is personally, can be used as a resource for others who may be disconnected from the Source.

"They are like bushes in the desert, living on salty ground where nothing else grows. Nothing good happens to them." (Jeremiah: 17:6) We can be channels of grace to others. Stay connected.

• Why is it important for you to remain connected to God?
• How could such connection affect your relationship with others, especially your partner?

Growth takes place one day at a time.

The Value Of Trade-Offs

In our marriage, it is rare that we are so complementary and agreeable that some form of negotiation or compromise is not needed. It is essential to work out trade-offs with each other. This allows us to do our thing because our partners are doing theirs.

When we begin to experience a one-sided effort on our part, we are probably close to some form of resentment and general unhappiness. There needs to be an understanding, hopefully by both, that a giving and receiving process must occur if the marriage is going to survive and grow. On occasion, there can spring up some severe differences and professional help may be necessary for successful resolution. This can be a plus for the relationship and the process of negotiation can progress and grow.

• What trade-offs occur in your marriage?
• How can good negotiation skills and the use of trade-offs
help your marriage?

Growth takes place one day at a time.

The Violence Within

We are reminded daily in the media of the violent world we live in. When it is in someone else's community, we may believe we have escaped the impact. Closer to home, most of us can, with some effort, recognize and identify scenes in which we have experienced our own inner violence.

Consider any time in which you experienced yourself resentful and angry. It may be our partner. It may have no connection with a direct violation of our rights. It may be as simple as someone getting into "our space." When that happens, we may say nothing but we feel a need to protect ourselves. There springs up within a sudden surge of negative feelings that we attempt to control or manage. Consider your own violence within and any of the triggers to those feelings that exist.

- *What feelings of aggression in yourself are you most aware of?*
- *How have you tried to deal with these feelings in your relationship with your partner?*

Growth takes place one day at a time.

Look For Some Good Things

Many of us grew up in an atmosphere of competitiveness, caution, and right and wrong. We tend to have limited focus on optimism, sharing, and encouragement. This focus, however, can enlarge when we give and receive more appreciation and encouragement.

One of the things we know about successful relationships is that there is a high rate of exchange of positives with each other. Some of us need time and our best effort to experience this in our relationship. Begin simply by reviewing the things you do for each other. What is the attitude that shows itself the most? How are these gestures received? What happens when they stop, even for a while? There may be a lot of real nice things happening in your relationship that you can become aware of. When you do, share a sign of appreciation.

- *What are some of the things you really like*
about your marriage?
- *How could an honest admission and appreciation of the good*
things in your marriage strengthen your love for each other?

Growth takes place one day at a time.

Seeds For Deeper Understanding

We marry for different reasons. It may be with the belief that marriage will somehow change our lives. We will finally be happy. This person will complete us and we will be content. Our emptiness will go away and we will be comforted and satisfied. It offers us the magic that will satisfy our needs. At least, this is what the lyrics in our popular songs would have us believe. This much seems certain, however, that our marriage is the fertile ground for a mysterious invasion of intense feelings calling for understanding and direction.

Into our marriage and in other very close, loving relationships, we bring our past experiences. When we appreciate these seemingly mysterious invasions as occurrences for mutual understanding, we can move in the direction of deeper respect for the many experiences we all bring into our relationships. The seeds have been planted and they need our nourishing attention.

- *How is appreciation and understanding of your past helpful to your marriage?*
- *How are you both currently dealing with those things you each brought to your marriage?*
- *What can you do to better understand and appreciate these influences upon your marriage relationship?*

Growth takes place one day at a time.

The Movements That Count

When we marry, we are willing to say "YES" to just about anything. For the present, everything is OK. The difficulty occurs when we expect to continue our "YES" and when others hold us to it indefinitely.

The times for saying "NO" arrive shortly. These are times when the "I" needs to move toward the "We." These are the times of discouragement, disappointment, and disillusionment. These are times necessary to say "NO" to that part of ourselves that needs to bear the burdens that occur in relating with each other intimately. Surrendering ourself is necessary for forming and nurturing a loving union. Without such willingness to surrender, we live with false securities and shallow fixes that only require more and more fixes. It is our openness to each other that lets in the love as we come to know the specialness of our union. This allows for the mature "YES" to evolve and flourish.

- *How difficult has it been for you to move from the "I" to the "We" in your marriage?*
- *What help along the way has been available for such a movement in your relationship to occur?*
- *How successful do you feel you are in strengthening the "We" without losing the "I"?*

Growth takes place one day at a time.

Aware Of Ourselves First

Because we are reluctant to consider our own history and our own problems, we tend to focus on our partner's contribution to the problem. We need to learn to resist this if we are going to avoid remaining stuck in our conflicts. We can benefit most by learning to look carefully at our own feelings and behavior. Of course, it is important and beneficial to learn how to respond to our partner, but we can never achieve the harmony we desire unless we are becoming aware and accepting of our own feelings.

Listen to what upsets you. Is the feeling you are having a familiar one? Is it in proportion to the situation you are in? Our challenge is to come to acknowledge that our partner's behavior is not the source of our unhappiness. When we change, our partner can and often does change.

- *Can you realistically admit the positive as well as the problematic contributions you bring to your marriage?*
- *How can such an open and honest admission help nurture your love and your marriage?*

Growth takes place one day at a time.

Risking To Share

The beauty and power of sharing lies in the openness to know and be known by our partner. Of course, such transparency can seem dangerous and difficult because of our own protections. We can, nevertheless, learn to trust when we become aware of each other's weaknesses. We can become sensitized to each other's feelings and the actions we express with each other. Our love can open us up to various depths in our relationship and break the bonds of our own restricted vision that comes from mutual weaknesses and problem areas.

When we shut ourselves off from our feelings of warmth or love in order to protect ourselves from perceived pain, we come to experience ourselves deprived of those very experiences we most need. This generates anger. The issue then becomes, not our anger, but what is stopping us from attachment. This issue is vital to understand in all of our loving relationships.

- *What risk do you experience when you are about to share yourself with your partner?*
- *What could your partner do to help reduce that risk for you?*

Growth takes place one day at a time.

Getting To Know You

How do we come to know other people? This is not just a theoretical question. We can gain a general knowledge about someone, a kind of broad understanding. We may also gain specific knowledge and understanding of people. They can tell us directly about themselves, of course.

We can also learn about them indirectly without them telling us anything. We receive vital information from what we see and hear. We don't have to limit our knowledge of each other. We just need to keep our eyes and ears open. We can learn a great deal from what is not put into words and not limit ourselves to the verbal only.

Are you getting to know each other better? What are you learning about each other? What is the main source for your knowing each other? Do you believe that you know all there is to know about each other?

•Do you really have each other figured out?
•Is there still a curiosity existing in your relationship?

Growth takes place one day at a time.

Courage Wins Out

It takes a lot of courage to live our life every day. The base meaning of the word courage comes from the Latin word *cor*-heart. In other words, it really takes heart. Implicit in all of this is the fact that there are very few areas in our life that do not involve taking risks. We take risks in our work, in our social life, in our marriage, in loving.

We need to encourage and be encouraged often. Are you encouraging each other or are you discouraging? Do you demand perfection of yourself and each other? Are you quick to find fault and pick out the little flaws instead of looking for the good in the efforts and intentions? Are you perhaps more subtle and attempt to do something for your partner when he or she is perfectly capable of doing it?

> • *What are some of the ways you can encourage each other?*
> • *How do you feel when you are encouraged?*

Growth takes place one day at a time.

Changes In Our Life

One of the most predictable elements in our life is change. It is inevitable, yet it is often difficult to accept in our personal life and our marriage. Few of us are prepared to accept the changes that come with time. We tend to accept something as dramatic as a crippling disease because in some way we can see it coming. The more subtle changes seem less tolerable. In fact, we may register mistrust and even disbelief when we experience another as appearing different in their views or actions.

Sometimes, we all need to be shocked out of our *rigor mortis,* a state that can set in after we are married a while. Our relationships need never remain static. We are either moving forward or backward.

•Consider the changes you are experiencing in your life and marriage.
• How are you dealing with them?

Growth takes place one day at a time.

Our Need For Others

Do you have a community of faith you can go to when you are in need? Do you ever feel guilty or ill at ease with the reality that you and your partner do not have any true friends? It is often easier to remain on the sideline, not get involved, to let the other couple do it, they are more experienced than we? Can you add to this list?

Belonging to a caring community, whether it is your church or synagogue or any other service group can be a true gift to others and to yourself. Each of us will have times of paralysis, physical and emotional. We can learn to trust in the help of others. They can, in turn, rely on the strength of our belief in them. Both form a workable combination.

- *What resources are available to you in your community that could help you grow as a person and as a couple?*
- *How could you personally and as a couple be a resource for others in your community?*

Growth takes place one day at a time.

Compassionate Listening

In the Old Testament, Moses appealed to God's compassion for himself and his people, even after having been angry and disillusioned with them for their lack of faithfulness and commitment. Jesus showed compassion for people by recognizing their needs and then simply requesting that they express what it is they wanted. He didn't second guess their requests or question their appropriateness at the time.

How do you express your compassion toward others, especially your partner? How do you read each other's needs? Can you allow yourself to recognize the needs as they arise with each other? Do you look for hidden agendas or question the motives of each other? Compassion does not second-guess. It recognizes and rewards honesty and straightforwardness. Can you express your needs directly? Are you compassionate with each other? Compassionate understanding is essential for listening to the deeper needs we all have.

> • *Share your thoughts and feelings with each other*
> *using the questions above.*

Growth takes place one day at a time.

The Ups And Downs

Despite the fact that we have come to know from experience that life goes on with many interruptions and that variety can be the spice of life, we nevertheless seek to control our ups and downs in life. There are those special moments when we feel good inside and we truly believe that somehow all is well even though we may be encountering discomfort and distress of one kind or the other.

We are inclined perhaps to turn back to those moments when we felt refreshed and hopeful to cling to those memories in which we experienced a peace and quiet that may now come less regularly and perhaps even seldom. What may be happening now for us is the call to "come down from the mountain top," "take our heads out of the clouds," "face the music," "walk in the desert." Joy is real and so is pain. We can experience both.

- *How would you translate the ups and downs
  in your relationship?*
- *What gives you strength and courage at the times
  of the downs?*
- *How do you help each other?*

Growth takes place one day at a time.

Our Weeds And Flowers

It is difficult to tell the difference between a weed and a planted flower in its early stage of growth. In fact, for some there is no difference except, we are told, in the eye of the beholder.

Similarly, it is difficult to view different aspects in our own lives. Viewing what in our lives is worthwhile and needing to be maintained and nourished is not always clear. Knowing what is useless or even damaging for our personal growth does not always prompt us to get rid of it. It takes us time to sort these things out in our life.

Asking ourselves what they are doing there, what contribution they are making to our health and welfare, should we be hanging on to them and what might happen if we disengage ourselves from them, are all challenging and disturbing questions to ask ourselves. Dare we ask them? How could such questions help your marriage relationship?

- *What in your personal life are you hanging on to that serves no positive purpose either to yourself or your marriage?*
- *How could letting these go help you and your marriage?*

Growth takes place one day at a time.

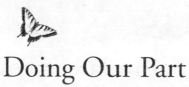

Doing Our Part

Back in the days when the milkman brought the milk to our door, there is a story of the little boy whose mother told him to bring in the milk from the porch. His mother noticed how tentative he seemed as he approached the door. It was just beginning to darken outside. Mother shouted out, "Don't worry, God's out there, it will be alright." Soon the boy shouted out, "God, if you're out there, bring in the milk."

Do we rely upon someone else to "bring us the milk?" Do we look to our partner to do something for us that we really can do for ourselves, thus building up a dependency that is unnecessary? This does not mean that we can't ask for someone to help us or lend a hand. It does mean that we ask ourselves if we are using the talent we have and seeking to overcome any of those fears that keep us from taking the risk and reaching out for what we want.

• Are you getting your needs and wants met?
• What could you do to help yourself?
• How could being more assertive help you in your marriage?

Growth takes place one day at a time.

A Formula For Peace

The Prayer of Francis of Assisi is a staunch reminder of what it is going to take to bring about the peace we so much yearn for. It will take our ability to bracket our own need to be consoled so we can console another; it means that it is going to be our willingness to try and understand when perhaps we are in need of understanding for ourselves; it is going to mean giving even a little bit more of ourselves when it would be so right and just to be on the receiving line; it also means that we cannot yet experience peace for ourselves until and unless we are willing to pardon the other. Finally, as the seed must die in order to become new life, so too we must die. We must change and allow ourselves to be changed if we seek true happiness.

These are strong words to listen to. This could be just what we need in order to be healed from the discord and disconnectedness in our marriage. Read Francis' prayer together.

> • *What are your thoughts and feelings regarding the words of St. Francis?*
> • *What are you willing to do to promote inner peace in yourself and peace in your marriage relationship?*

Growth takes place one day at a time.

Our Sexual Intimacy

When it comes to sex, is "normalcy" still being defined as "whatever is thought, felt or performed by the majority?" If so, then most of us can hardly be found in that category. There is no absolute standard against which we can measure our sex, either in frequency or in quality. There could be complications and even medical abnormalities such as diseased genitals or pathological fear. Assuming these are not present, the questions of how pleasurable, and how often, pertaining to our sexual intimacy can only be answered by us.

We need to place more confidence in our own judgment and evaluation in this personal matter of our marriage sex. The experts, TV personalities, the mass media and social customs and traditions have to be interpreted through our own needs, wants and values. The when, how, how often and the quality is up to each of us to determine.

- *How important is your sexual intimacy to you?*
- *How do you make known your sexual wants to each other?*
- *How are your attitudes alike? How are they different?*

Growth takes place one day at a time.

A Cooperative Venture

Most of us believe we know what it takes to make a successful marriage. We may even know a couple or two who seem to have it all together. The fact of the matter is, however, that we are not given a private tour into each other's marriage and we probably have encountered a surprise or two when we hear that so and so is getting a divorce.

A stable and satisfying relationship is an ideal we reach for. Most of the time our backgrounds going into marriage are quite dissimilar and even if they do resemble each other, there are no guarantees. Our cooperative efforts seem essential and our ability to work as a team is still considered to be vital for our efforts to pay off.

• Are you functioning as a team? If so, great.
• If not, what is needed from each of you that would
help you obtain a more mutual effort making
your relationship what you want it to be?

Growth takes place one day at a time.

The Benefits Are Mutual

When we express our caring for each other we receive certain benefits in return. Just as when we truly listen to another and the other experiences a boost in their self-esteem, so too, when we care for another in whatever ways we do that, we experience something new happening within us. We grow, we feel better about ourselves, we experience a change in ourselves that we had not planned for.

When we care, we run the risk of the unknown. This takes a lot of courage and trust in the other person and ourselves. We may find ourselves in unchartered waters and we become open and sensitive to what happens in the present. Caring by itself is sufficient to promote growth in each other. This takes courage. Consider the different opportunities you have for caring for each other.

- *In what ways do you express caring to your partner?*
- *How do you experience being cared for by your partner?*

Growth takes place one day at a time.

The Gift Of Silence

One of our greatest teachers in life is "Silence." "What a strange power there is in silence! How many resolutions are formed, how many sublime conquests affected, during that pause when lips are closed, and the soul secretly feels the touch of her maker upon her! They are the strong ones of the earth who know how to keep silence when it is a pain and grief unto them, and who give time to their own souls to wax strong against temptation?" -Emerson.

Emerson reminds us of how much we need silence in our life in order to remain in touch with the deeper needs within and to contact our God. Carlyle puts it this way, "Silence is the element in which great things fashion themselves together." Only in silence will certain things emerge from within. Take the time to go within and be silent. There is much for you to learn there. Be patient in your efforts to get there.

• How comfortable are you with the silences in your life?
• How could you use silence to reach the deeper needs within yourself and your relationship?

Growth takes place one day at a time.

The Unselfishness In Love

When all is said and done, it is loving and being loved that really counts. It is in being able to want what is best for another, it is in being able to relate to what is truly in their best interest, that we really care for others. This requires an ability to bracket my needs at times so I can listen to yours. It requires a certain selflessness.

When we do this for each other and extend ourselves, we experience something special happening to us at the same time. We experience an inner peace, and a sense of importance and fulfillment while not directly seeking it for ourselves. This can be one of those "miracles" in our relationships. As we reach out, we experience something special returning back to us. Consider how this might occur for you in your marriage.

> • *How does your love for your partner involve*
> *the giving of yourself?*
> • *How do you experience generosity in your partner's expression*
> *of love toward you?*

Growth takes place one day at a time.

Turning To Our Intentions

Intentions are very powerful forces in determining where we are and where we are going. They focus our actions. They also play a vital role in clarifying our communication. When we clarify our intentions with our partner, our communication can be better understood and we lessen the chances of conflict and misunderstanding.

When we get in touch with our intentions and when we can express these clearly, we add to our ability to make known the deeper and more honest parts of ourselves. Asking each other his/her intentions in certain conversations can bring to light the reason for saying what we say. When we ask ourselves exactly what we intend, we can communicate clearly and increase the success of our communication with each other. Consider how your intentions play a role in your communications with your partner.

- *How are your intentions expressed in your communication with each other?*
- *What advantages are there in identifying and understanding your intentions?*

Growth takes place one day at a time.

Loving That Person

Someone once said, "I love everybody–it's people I can't stand." The fact of the matter is that we can't love everybody and attempting to do so is energy placed in the wrong direction. The real challenge seems to occur when we focus our attention on this or that specific person. We may be able to care in general but we need to consider specific persons in our life. A general intention based on goodwill is insufficient.

Just as we need to be able to care for the other, we need to evaluate how we go about caring and how that person responds to our caring. We can ask our partner how he/she experiences our caring, thus learning specific needs and ways to care for that person in our life. This can help us direct our caring energies in a meaningful way with each other. Learning how our partner would like us to express love to him or her can be helpful.

- *How can you tell when your loving caring is being accepted by your partner?*
- *How do you and your partner assess your caring needs?*

Growth takes place one day at a time.

No Replacements Please

Replacements may be necessary for various objects around the house, but they never work in a relationship. We need to know, with consistency, that our partner is here and available. It is this consistency that allows for the development of such necessary elements in our marriage as trust and commitment. Dependability adds to the strength of the relationship.

We foster this constancy when we send frequent signals to each other that say, "I am here," "I am here for you," "I notice you," "I know you are here," "I know you are here for me," "We are here for each other." We need to know and we need to hear this often from each other. This strengthens and reinforces our commitment. It is not based on the fear of losing the other. It is based on the fact that we care for each other. It is another one of those ways of expressing our love.

• How is your partner present for you?
• Is there a consistency in your presence and availability for each other?

Growth takes place one day at a time.

Structuring Our Time

There are different ways we can spend our time. We may take time for ourselves to follow a personal interest or hobby on our fun. We may pursue this hobby in the presence of the other, but still separately, such as when one is reading and the other is watching TV. Both are in the same room but engaged in different activities.

Another way we spend our time is when we are together in some form of interaction, whether in conversation, a heated emotional exchange or making love. Often there is an imbalance and our emphasis may be in one of the three areas or one may be excluded altogether. There are different combinations and often it can be helpful to know just where we are in our relationship.

> *• What difficulties do you encounter attempting to have time alone, and time together?*
> *• Is there an acceptable balance involving time alone and time together?*
> *• What percentage of time do you spend in each of the three structures?*

Growth takes place one day at a time.

Another Side Of Guilt

Guilt can wear different masks. It has become the target of many who seek to explore its secrets. It can be non-productive, painful and neurotic.

When we identify, understand and direct it, it can be very helpful in guiding us to causes for our failures and help get us back on track. It does not have to be our enemy. It can point to error in our judgment. It can signal neglect and indifference in our relationship. It can serve as a guide when it calls us back to commitments, promises and old intentions. It can call us to evaluate and assess where we are and where we are going in our marriage. We can learn from our guilt.

- *What significance does guilt have for you?*
- *Does guilt carry any message that could be helpful for you, for your relationship?*

Growth takes place one day at a time.

We May Be Missing Someone

This is not so much a question that seeks a spontaneous response as it is a question of awareness. Are we really in touch with the needs of others around us? Are our time and our efforts so directed and focused that we are unable to listen for the needs coming from those close to us? What may occur is that we notice we are not reaching out. We no longer express concern. We may even use the old slogan, "Well, that's the way things are nowadays."

Now, let's look at some possible reactions: Is there someone you promised to contact but never have; is there a phone call that you need to make; is there something left undone that needs to be completed? Some prayerful consideration can provide more awareness and help us to respond courageously. Listen carefully to yourself on this one. Your action patterns can help you in your awareness.

- *What are you doing personally to remain in contact with the people that are important to you?*
- *What are you doing together to rekindle and foster relationships with other couples?*

Growth takes place one day at a time.

When Roles Are Unclear

At times we may become aware of our inability to get along. Conflicts occur in which we compare ourselves with each other. We experience a sense of futility and competition. We may not even be aware of the competitiveness except for the thoughts of not measuring up, either to our own expectations or of our partner. Our roles, at the time, may seem unclear and the smoothness of a give-and-take simply does not occur. We tend to argue and "duke" it out over some of the simplest things.

Often, who is in charge is crucial. When we can decide this issue, it seems that other things fall into place and we can often get away from the "who is right and who is wrong" judgment calls. Are there tasks that one of you can lead in and the other follow? Identifying these may be helpful.

- *What are the roles that have been assigned or simply assumed in your marriage relationship?*
- *How have you experienced each other in these roles?*

Growth takes place one day at a time.

Support With Reassurance

In the Old Testament, in Judges, Gideon is asked to do a task. He recognizes his inadequacies and pleads to be excused. God simply tells him that He will be with him. Gideon finally accepts the task and then expresses more doubts. This again reflects his lack of belief and his need for reassurance.

Don't we often experience need for reassurance even when we believe we have finally given our true assent to pick up the task and go with it? Even then, we find ourselves experiencing new doubts about the task or even our ability to do the task. We need reassurance on our journey. We have chosen our pathway but we need help along the way. Let's admit our doubts and our inadequacies and still remain in our journey, confident that "God is with us." Spend some time with each other and express how each of you need support and reassurance on your journey together.

> • *How would you like that support given to you*
> *by your partner?*
> • *How do you make your needs for support and reassurance*
> *known to each other?*

Growth takes place one day at a time.

A Time For Centering

At some time we may ask ourselves the question whether it is possible to have singleness of purpose. Can we really keep our hands steady on the plow and heading in a clear direction? Most of us live a scattered life. We focus on our work, then our home life, then our social life. Our life becomes fragmented. We go from one to the other. We leave behind little pieces of ourselves. It is difficult to respond equally to all the demands, needs and invitations that come our way.

We need to maintain our inner peace. We need to make time each day, to go inside and be at peace knowing God is present and that we are here open to His presence. These moments become our silent opportunity for acknowledging who we are and where we are. This is holy ground. This place you are in right now is a place of inner peace. "Be still and wait." (Psalm 37:7)

> • *What can you do to bring about a centering in your life?*
> • *How could such personal centering help you*
> *and affect your relationship?*

Growth takes place one day at a time.

Little Things Mean A Lot

It is easy to minimize the small things and maximize the large ones. What about the times we prevent a major conflict from erupting because we stopped the argument from escalating at the very beginning? What of the times when the healing begins with the simple words, "I'm sorry" or "Please forgive me" or "Can we talk about it?"

These are major steps taken in our relationship when we pay attention and take credit for those little starts, those small efforts that "nip the situation in the bud." The large miracles in our life seldom, if ever, happen. It is those little miracles, those seemingly little things that we are doing that bring about the little healings and the accumulation of little bright spots in our marriage. These mean so much and contribute to the health and satisfaction we experience. Don't underestimate those little efforts you are making with each other. They count for a lot.

- *What are some of the little things you are doing to help make your relationship more satisfying?*
- *What are some other little ways you could help enrich and strengthen your relationship?*

Growth takes place one day at a time.

Time To Review And Renew

Our marital commitments are seldom renewed or reviewed. For whatever reason, we push on attempting to do our best and hope for the pieces of our life to fall into place. Some of us are more invested in our efforts to direct the course of our life and we renew and review.

Strengthening our commitment is essential. We can take time to review where we are in terms of how we are meeting our own and each other's needs. We may want to focus on a particular area of our relationship and avoid the general or cursory glance that goes nowhere. We may choose to take inventory of our relationship covering the last six months or the last year. However we choose to do it, reviewing our commitment can lead to renewal and revitalize our marriage. It can be just what we need to help us stay on track.

> • *Review these areas in light of their affect on your marriage relationship over a period of time.*
> • *How could such periodic reviews help you and your relationship?*

Growth takes place one day at a time.

Maintaining Our Aliveness

One of the powerful forces affecting our growth as couple is our own personal growth, the necessity of being true to ourselves. We care enough about ourselves to listen to our own awarenesses. We cannot be for another if we cannot also be for ourselves.

Can you tell your partner that you will do all you can to stay physically, mentally, emotionally and spiritually alive? This is a big question and a big answer to give to each other. This is a large promise but it is really all any of us can promise. We cannot predict the future. We cannot say how we will feel twenty years from now. We can only attempt to maintain ourselves as best we can. The honesty that this promotes lies in the admission and acceptance of our own personal contribution to maintaining aliveness in our marriage. As individuals, we alone can do this. It is that special loving gift that we can give to each other.

- *What are you personally doing to stay healthy and alive?*
- *What support can you give each other that would encourage personal growth and aliveness in your marriage?*

Growth takes place one day at a time.

Honoring Our Promises

Most of us consider our promises to others as serious business. We weigh the results of keeping our promises against the repercussions of breaking them and choose the course likely to cause us the least amount of difficulty.

But what about those many little promises we make to ourselves? Do we treat them with the same respect and seriousness? We promise ourselves we will take better care of our health or undertake some project that we know could benefit us personally. Do we hold ourselves responsible for these as well? Frequently, we dismiss these and do not hold ourselves responsible to ourselves. This, of course, does not mean we should badger ourselves with guilt or condemnation. It does mean, however, that we consider whether we discount the importance of ourselves and the importance of those promises. It is vital to reward ourselves when we keep those promises.

- *What promises are you making to yourself?*
- *Do these promises reflect a personal goal or desire?*
- *How do you feel when you honor these personal promises to yourself? What happens when you do not keep them?*

Growth takes place one day at a time.

A Focused Direction

Knowingly or unknowingly, our philosophy of life directs and orders our life. To be and live as a caring person is a powerful focus. Rather than limit us, it gives a direction to our life that could otherwise be drab and limited. Caring can direct and coordinate our inner forces, like an artist who disciplines himself in order to produce his artwork. Caring directs our intentions, values and activities. In turn, we attract other caring people to us.

· Our caring serves as a guiding light along our daily paths. It becomes active after awhile without consciously intending it. Of course, along the way we may need to renew our decision to be care givers. It uniquely excludes what is incompatible to caring and allows us to unfold and emerge from within ourselves.

• What directs and orders your life?
• Is there a direction and order for your relationship?
• How could you be care givers to each other?

Growth takes place one day at a time.

Our Journey Together

It is easy to believe that when we marry we will simply enter into oneness and form a complete union. Many books, songs and people attempt to convince us it is so. The fact is that we will struggle with "me" and "we" throughout our entire marriage. How much is for me and how much is for us? How much can I be without separating myself from you? How much can we be us without being swallowed up in the process and losing my precious individuality and uniqueness?

This is the basic challenge for all of us who are married. This challenge remains throughout our life and it requires time to be worked with patiently, carefully and lovingly. A union of short duration cannot accomplish this. Our commitment to each other is truly vital.

- *How separate and unique do you experience yourself in your marriage?*
- *How together and joined do you feel in your marriage?*

Growth takes place one day at a time.

Keeping Our Vision Clear

Ideally in our marriage we are looking and going in the same direction. Our vision is clear. The energy is directed and uncluttered. This is hardly true for most of us, though it could be true for a time.

The reality is that not only can our vision become cloudy, but the energy we put into our marriage can often become unbalanced. A working collaboration is difficult to achieve and sustain. There may be a situation where we act totally together as a team. An example of this could be our mutual dedication in caring for a very ill child.

• Do you have a clear vision for your marriage?
• Do you ever talk about what you want your marriage to be
as you make your journey together?
• Where are you placing your energy and is your marriage
getting its fair share?

Growth takes place one day at a time.

Maintaining Our Perspective

Our work can be very important to us. In fact, it may be the most important part of our life judging by the time, effort and attention we give it. We are told by some eager motivators that it "has" to become "the" most important pathway if we want to succeed and get ahead. This really depends upon our definition of success. Work can be considered a spiritual path for us. But it can be only one path. We have others.

Our family, our marriage, our leisure time are all paths to being successful because these are all part of a healthy balance in our life. Spirituality and health call for balance.

•What are the main paths in your life and in your marriage and where does work fit into the balance?
• Do your choices reflect the direction you are going as an individual and as a couple?

Growth takes place one day at a time.

Discovering Along The Way

In our courtship and in our marriage, we come to know about our partner. But knowing about him or her is not the same as being present to that person. We can be drawn into a genuine relationship before we really know much about him or her. This may occur during a crisis, a time of great joy, or by observing and experiencing that person over a longer period of time. A way of looking, certain gestures, attractive mannerisms, and an engaging personality can capture our attention, and we are on our way. Knowing about that person seems secondary.

Love invites us to know more. To know about his or her past, friends, feelings, opinions. This can lead to delicious discoveries! Learning new things about each other in our marriage is not just assembling a biographical file. It is building on little discoveries each day and recognizing them and confirming them lovingly.

- *What have you recently discovered about your partner?*
- *How open are you to the mysterious qualities and surprises of your partner?*
- *How could such discoveries contribute to joy and excitement in your relationship?*

Growth takes place one day at a time.

Failings In Our Love

Love has its lapses. It may even be lost. There are times when we say we can no longer love even when we really do. Sound complicated? It can be. These are the moments when we are most apt to consider leaving. We may feel that we have already left emotionally. We just haven't walked yet.

Every child at some time wants to run away from home. We, as adults, have our moments too—what fills the gap when we experience our love lapsing? Can a firm religious or civil law keep us in place? It could. Can guilt settle us down? Maybe. All these could simply provide another reason for the absence of love. Could it be that the remedy is love itself? A love that is better understood and given a realistic chance to succeed.

- *What changes have you experienced in your love for each other since marriage?*
- *How have you attempted to deal with these changes?*
- *In what ways has your love become more realistic and honest?*

Growth takes place one day at a time.

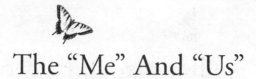

The "Me" And "Us"

I have always had difficulty accepting at face value the advice "let your feelings all hang out," "let everyone know where you are at," "look out for number one." In particular, these statements reflect a preoccupation with one's rights and self-interest without adequately recognizing the importance of others. I have no difficulty accepting the need for defining one's boundaries and the right to express those boundaries. When this does not foster intimacy and trust in a relationship, and cuts off the possibility of meaningful dialogue, then it appears to be self-serving and harmful to the relationship. There is much in our society that rewards our preoccupation with the self, me and I. True self-esteem values the self without making it a tower preoccupied with the task of warding off all intruders.

- *How freely do you express your thoughts and feelings to each other?*
- *How responsible are you for the results that flow from the expression of those feelings?*

Growth takes place one day at a time.

Feeling Loved

"That's not what I need." These are hard words to listen to when we have just worked so hard to make the other happy. We purchased a gift, rendered a service, went out of our way, just so we could do something "nice." Of course, we didn't bother to ask, somewhere along the line, if our offering is what is really needed or wanted.

When our partner says he or she does not feel loved, this can be a personal and honest admission without us immediately declaring our guilt. We need to discover the reason for what is happening before planning our course to "fix" it. This is particularly difficult when our experience in our relationship tells us that we are receiving some of what we need, but something else is missing. With honesty and growing awareness of our deepest needs, we can gradually come to expressing these needs. Do I feel loved? Do you feel loved? Difficult question to ask yourself and your partner.

> • *What are the times when you feel unloved?*
> • *What is your ability to talk to each other regarding your needs and wants?*

Growth takes place one day at a time.

Look Ahead

An old biblical injunction of not sending in soldiers to fight twice and three times your number is sound advice. Attempting to make peace in advance is an appropriate and smart maneuver. Of course, leaving the scene may be admirable and wise as well.

In your marriage you can help yourself by anticipating certain scenes, reactions and problems. The old story of "if I know in advance, I will make it come true," does not magically work. When we are prepared, we acknowledge possibilities and we can engage in a meaningful dialogue about those possibilities occurring, especially if they have a habit of repeating themselves. This gives us a certain safe distance to talk and act together. The experience also allows us to feel some necessary control over our lives and the problem situations we become involved in. Anticipating the problem areas occurring in your relationship can be helpful in growing together peacefully.

- *What reactions from your partner can you anticipate?*
- *How could anticipating certain events and reactions in your relationship help you in your marriage?*

Growth takes place one day at a time.

Changing Attitudes

"I always knew I would go to school, get married and have a family." For some of us, our vision was quite clear and certain. We assumed the other person in our life would be clear and certain also. For many of us, such was not the case. In our relationships, we either live happily with the differences, or we become miserable indeed.

An appreciation for differing attitudes and expectations can go a long way. It often comes down to the recognition that we may change our views on marriage, the longer we remain married. This changing attitude can be related to our personal growth as we become older and face the changing realities in our lives. Our marriage can and does evolve as we move along our journey.

- *Can you identify any changing attitudes in your marriage relationship?*
- *How have these changes in attitude, since your marriage, affected your relationship with each other?*

Growth takes place one day at a time.

Realistic Expectations

Unrealistic expectations can cause dissatisfaction, frustration and conflict in our relationships. These expectations may be expressed directly and indirectly. "You must take care of me," "Be the first to apologize when we argue," "Be the disciplinarian in our home," "Include me in all your activities." Can you add any here that you are aware of in yourself and your marriage? How realistic are they? Assess your expectations and how they are active in your relationship.

Our love does not entitle us to impose unrealistic expectations and control over our partner. Some of our expectations are realistic and appropriate. What are these, and can you review these with each other? With mutual encouragement, you can assess those expectations that help or harm your relationship.

- *What expectations did you bring to your marriage and can you identify the specific areas involved?*
- *How have these expectations affected your relationship?*

Growth takes place one day at a time.

Loosen Up Control

There is something attractive in the strong injunction, "make it happen," especially when it comes from within our own head. We become ready to challenge, confront and change things. We feel in control and our mission is to conquer, stay on top, gather all the data and overcome the obstacles.

There is, of course, the strong possibility that we overlook the natural flow of certain things in our lives. We can disallow for the natural progression and process that simply requires its own pace and time. Sometimes we become impatient, restless and edgy over the unmastered areas in our marriage relationship. Just as there seems to be a personal rhythm, there is also a relational rhythm we can attempt to understand and appreciate. Perhaps you have experienced that side of the rhythm when you feel tranquil, contented, loving, relaxed, calm, pleased, assured and thankful.

- *How important is it for you to be in control?*
- *In what areas does this show up the most?*
- *How is control expressed in your relationship?*

Growth takes place one day at a time.

Grooving In A Rut

The routines we set up, whether at work or play, can be assuring and gratifying. They render a certain assurance and predictability that many of us like. In our marriage, however, certain routines, over time, can make us restless and bored. Webster defined a "rut" as "a way of life so fixed in routine as to be dreary." Our commitments to certain activities may be lessening because that activity no longer is appealing or gratifying. In other words, these activities are grooved and we may be experiencing restlessness and boredom.

We may also have specific routines at home and structure our time and interest to limit ourselves to remain more at home. It becomes more and more difficult to get dressed to go out. We find no outside activity able to interest us or give us pleasure. The results could include a decline in our verbal and emotional exchange with each other.

> • *Are you grooving yourselves into marriage routines?*
> • *How can you help prevent boredom from setting into your marriage relationship?*

Growth takes place one day at a time.

Lovers Do Not Judge

Blaming is a form of psychological name calling. It is perfectly within our right to question why our partner does what he or she does. This certainly is preferable to playing the mind reading game. It is unreasonable to tell our partners they do not know what "they" are saying or feeling. It is just as harmful to our relationship when we diagnose each other. You're a "mama's boy," "you just want to hurt me," "you're just trying to get even." Such comments are verbal hostility and never helpful. Our partner does not want to be judged and neither do we.

Listen carefully to understand so your partner can share openly. When it is your turn, your partner will be there because he or she will have experienced your loving caring and listening.

- *Do you blame and judge each other?*
- *How could you move from judging to understanding what your partner does and says?*
- *How could this benefit you and your marriage relationship?*

Growth takes place one day at a time.

Making Our Needs Known

It is not easy for some of us to express our needs, to make known verbally what it is we want and need. We therefore rely upon caution, carefulness and sometimes silence itself to cushion our expression of those wants and needs. Underlying all of this is our fear. This may be fear of something terrible happening to us. Others will laugh at us or even judge our needs and wants as bad and unacceptable.

Some of our needs are quite basic and refer to needs we had as children, the need for love, acceptance and security. When these are not met adequately in our childhood, they tend to reappear when we are adults. It is important that we not wait until a crisis occurs before we spill out our needs and wants. This will take some practice and a lot of patience with ourselves and each other. Begin today to acknowledge and then express what it is you want and need.

- *How do you express your needs and wants to each other?*
- *How do you respond to each other's expression of these needs and wants?*

Growth takes place one day at a time.

Attentive To Each Other

Distractions come and go. When they linger they suggest disinterest, inattentiveness and even rudeness. Attentiveness to your partner is reassuring, sensitive and loving. Looking elsewhere, walking away, changing the subject, looking preoccupied with something else when your partner is talking can send negative messages. When it becomes a habitual response it can contribute to hurt feelings and distancing from each other.

It is often difficult to recognize when we are being inattentive. We can choose to be honest and say, "I'm, sorry honey, I didn't hear what you said... I was distracted... will you repeat what you said?" We all can appreciate this kind of honesty rather than act as if we heard when we really didn't. Being attentive to each other is a powerful ingredient in your relationship. It really deserves your attention from time to time.

- *Are you aware of how you are inattentive to your partner?*
- *What are some ways you express this inattentiveness?*
- *How can you become more attentive to the thoughts, feelings, needs and wants of your partner?*

Growth takes place one day at a time.

Thanks For Everything

We have heard it probably said it ourselves -"There are no guarantees in life." Whatever the circumstances or our reasons, we may still have difficulty believing it is true. Maybe we observed or we ourselves experienced a painful divorce or separation. The times we live in contain sweeping changes and we may hasten to the high lands for security, only to realize that escape and withdrawal offer little shelter.

Acknowledging our personal struggles and how we try to make our marriage work can provide a background for a deeper appreciation of what is stable, meaningful and non-negotiable in our marriage. Our society continues to shift and we must learn to adapt to certain changes as we sift through the meaning of it all. Today is appreciation day—time to offer a simple thanks to each other for whatever we feel grateful for in our relationship.

- *Tell each other one thing in your life you are grateful for.*
- *Tell each other one thing in your relationship you are grateful for.*

Growth takes place one day at a time.

Our Dependency Needs

As adults, we often experience needs, feelings and behaviors having their origins in our childhood. One of these is our dependency on others. We all, of course, are dependent in some way on someone. This does not mean that we are unable to function on our own in particular areas of our lives. In fact, it may be quite situational and separate from our professional or business life.

When we experience our separations or inability to form meaningful relationships as catastrophic and debilitating, we may be experiencing an overdependency problem. In an overdependency, we risk the loss of our individuality and identity. This often leads to depression, anxiety and shame. The solution is not to "keep a stiff upper lip." As with all efforts to grow as persons and as couples, we begin with a clear recognition and exploration of our needs and wants.

• In what ways do you need each other?
• Is there an overdependency in your relationship? If so, how?
• How can a mutual dependency be a natural process in your marriage relationship?

Growth takes place one day at a time.

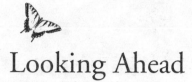

Looking Ahead

We need order in our society. Chaos can't be tolerated for very long. Married life is no different. A certain predictability of behavior, thoughts and feelings is required and expected by us. Our expectations of each other may differ in each marriage but some form of predictability provides stability and security.

When there is too much predictability and when everything is methodically ordered, there is little room for flexibility and spontaneity. Our marriage can become stilted and boring. Knowing what to expect and then dealing with what occurs often calls for transition skills of some kind. A new child arrives, a job transfer occurs, a relocation, death or illness.

- *What degree of predictability do you have and expect in your marriage?*
- *In what way does your marriage relationship benefit when predictability and clear expectations exist?*

Growth takes place one day at a time.

Uniquely Ours

Religions have referred to the marriage union in terms of a spiritual bond, a connection with God, a transcendent closeness. Our marriage reflects each of us as individuals and goes beyond both of us. It contains the seed of preservation while engaging in a dynamic movement into the future. Through time and so many shared events, we develop and nurture our own rituals, habits and traditions. As a couple, we continue to develop a system, a union uniquely our own.

While pursuing our individual needs and wants, we are also forming a common purpose to which we contribute our own unique personality and gifts. With chosen traditions that we take from our own family background, we form a unique marriage that we continue to create as our own.

• How unique and special do you feel?
• How unique and special do you feel you are to each other?
*• What are some of the unique qualities, charactistics you
brought with you to your marriage?*

Growth takes place one day at a time.

Our Need For Security

There can exist numerous threats to our security. Some come from the outside as in the loss of a job, a severe illness or accident. These could, and often do, bring a couple closer together. In a crisis, we tend to join forces and work toward a common goal. The result is often a more intimate and sharing relationship.

Threats can come from inside the marriage such as violence toward our partner, severe anger and mood swings. Less dramatic perhaps, but no less alarming are the references to dissatisfaction with our relationship or remarks reflecting an interest outside the marriage—working late hours, uninvolvement in family activities, frequent fights. The message that comes through is "I will leave you." Our need for security is reasonable and essential. Consider its meaning for you.

- *In what areas of your marriage relationship do you feel most secure?*
- *In what areas do you feel most insecure?*
- *What can you do to help each other feel reasonably secure with each other?*

Growth takes place one day at a time.

Wanting Approval

Understanding our own need for approval can help us in our efforts to support a realistic and loving relationship. Wanting approval is sensible and realistic for all of us. Needing approval, however, is something else. It springs from the mythical belief that we cannot survive and be happy without it. This is the message that relates to our belief in approval as a need. A way to combat this myth is to have inner confidence and a high regard for who we are.

Disapproval when given in a non-judgmental way can hurt, but it can also provide a powerful learning experience. We probably have close relatives and friends who tell us what we enjoy hearing. Listen to those you live with, especially your partner. Evaluate your need for approval.

• How is approval expressed in your marriage?
• How is disapproval expressed in your marriage?

Growth takes place one day at a time.

A Recollection Of Celebrations

In a recent church bulletin I read of the upcoming ceremonies for couples choosing to renew their marriage vows. Some are jubilarians. It seems quite natural to think of personal experiences with memories reaching back to family celebrations and parents' marriage.

I thought of how lucky we were back then. Mom and Dad celebrated sixty years of marriage. What a testimony to love and dedication. I couldn't help wondering if in some ways they had it easier. Our society has changed so much. The media, pressure from our work, the accent on equality and personal happiness all contribute to this change. There certainly are differences. My parents made it over the long haul. They may have questioned their relationship, but there was a certainty that invited respect and gratefulness. It was their solidarity, their staunchness, their determination that make me ever grateful and challenged. Does this prompt any memories and feelings for you?

- *What was celebrated in your home when you were growing up?*
- *How were people and events celebrated?*
- *What is there in your parents' marriage that you feel grateful for and in some way challenged?*

Growth takes place one day at a time.

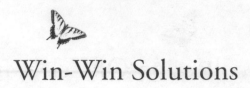

Win-Win Solutions

Going after the issue is virtually impossible when we are in a blistering argument and heavily invested in being right. We waste little time attempting to score points and push back the opposition. It may surprise us, even a little, how self-righteous we can become. Our justification is in our right to mobilize all the forces we can, in favor of the truth. What often follows, however, are words that wound and behaviors that scare and intimidate.

To win is really to lose as we usually discover not too far down the line. The truth is that we need for both to win to stop short of saying or doing things that leave a bad taste in our mouths. Most of it comes down to personal priorities, values, choices and feelings anyway. Consider your need to be right.

• *How important is it for both of you to be winners?*
• *How can your disagreements and arguments become learning experiences for both of you?*

Growth takes place one day at a time.

Being Authentic

We live in a world where imitations are passed off as substitutes for the authentic. In certain instances involving jewelry, we may deliberately choose the item knowing it is imitation. With certain other things, we will settle only for the real thing. We acknowledge easily the appeal of authenticity, especially when it comes to people. Being authentic is being real–free to be ourselves and able to live within the boundaries of truth, respect and love.

Every day in some way we are exposed to people and situations where our authenticity and realness is on the line. It can be at work or in our relationships.

Are you able to be who you are and not have to prove anything about yourself? Your ability to be who you are and live your life with freedom and authenticity is a wonderful tribute to a healthy life and marriage.

- *How authentic and real can you be in your marriage?*
- *How do you attempt to express your realness to each other?*
- *Are there any obstacles to being authentic and real in your relationship?*

Growth takes place one day at a time.

August 22

Loving Ingredients

Since I decided to personally maintain our lawn several years ago, I have learned a lot about lawn care. For one, too much of a good thing, even an essential thing, can contribute to bad results. I meant well and after all, fertilizer is necessary, right? The ground does send its own message in its own way, and I learned by observation, assessing, trial and error. In a very real sense, our marriage requires daily maintenance.

Make an effort to observe, listen and check out with each other. Learn from each other. These are vital ingredients for creating the loving and vibrant relationship you want for yourself and your partner.

- *Can you make known your needs and wants to each other without the use of any camouflage?*
- *Do you give what your partner wants and needs, or do you decide and hope for the best?*

Growth takes place one day at a time.

Free To Explore

A secretary quit her job because she experienced great difficulty accepting the communicating style of her bosses. Their style was to explore thoughts and options vigorously in her presence. She perceived this as noisy, unclear and going nowhere.

In a marriage, such a style consists of a tentative language and a search for understanding. For some of us, such a style can be productive and very valuable. Stifling such openness to explore could block thoughts and feelings from being expressed. A cousin to this is the fear that disagreement will only magnify our differences and undermine the marriage. Our differences are real. When we respect these differences and express them naturally, we learn from each other and we energize our relationship. Are you free in this area?

• Can you explore thoughts and feelings with each other?
• How could such exploration help you grow together
as a couple?

Growth takes place one day at a time.

The Bottom Line

I recently discovered the reason for my disappointment over the way I negotiated the selling price of our car. I had no bottom line. In marriage, there is a bottom line. It differs with each marriage, but it must be there. It consists of certain fundamentals we hold essential for the survival of our marriage. There may be room for negotiation on this or that, but on the bottom line there is no tampering. These fundamental principles hold the marriage together through thick and thin. On occasion they may need to be spelled out directly to each other. The experts list them as the necessity of a commitment, intimacy and prioritizing each other.

- *What is the bottom line for your marriage?*
- *Are they the same for you and your partner?*

Growth takes place one day at a time.

Risk To Be Ourselves

It takes courage to be ourselves. Not only to perform, but to be who we truly are. Courage is linked closely with risk and the fear of failure is ever present. Without risk, however, and the courage to be ourselves, we can become for others and risk losing ourselves in the process.

It is a risk to say, "that feels good, this does not," "when you do that I feel sad," "I am bored," "I want to be close but I don't want sex." There are changes necessary for us to make that call for risks to be taken. They reflect the true freedom we have to be ourselves. Change is difficult and often scary. Courage empowers us to risk the fear to be ourselves.

• How free are you to be yourself?
• Are you promoting this freedom in each other
to risk and be true to yourselves?

Growth takes place one day at a time.

Revealing Ourselves

It can be awfully tough to let down our guard. We want so badly for someone, especially our partner, to see through our protections, and to do so gently and carefully without hurting us. It is so difficult to feel vulnerable. Our inner refuge from pain, harm and misunderstanding is at stake. We need to feel safe, secure and trusting. This can overcome our fear because we are able to create an atmosphere in which we can communicate heart-to-heart with each other.

What weaknesses do you hide from your partner? We are all weak and vulnerable in our own way. Revealing yourself to your partner is a slow but rewarding process. This is where the little miracles happen. You discover that the more of your personality you reveal and is accepted, the more deeply loved you feel.

- *What is necessary for you to reveal yourselves to each other?*
- *How could such a process add to your intimacy with each other?*

Growth takes place one day at a time.

Respecting Each Other's Possessions

In a well-functioning relationship, we respect each other's possessions. This involves a clear definition of personal and joint ownership. The value of the items in our possession are determined by each partner alone and together.

Often when we marry, we bring with us items that hold special memories and meaning. Permission is needed before a decision is made to use or get rid of some item of property. Some items may be protected by a specific legal process. In some remarriages, for instance, there often is a legal process that specifies and binds both in certain ways.

Some things are protected by mutual understanding and agreement. This can be just as binding for some of us. Respecting each other's personal values and attachments is of significant importance to a well functioning relationship.

- *What arrangements, attitudes, understanding and feelings can you identify in regard to your personal and joint possessions?*
- *How do your responses affect your respect for each other?*

Growth takes place one day at a time.

Unmet Needs And Wants

The positive needs we have often go unmet. We may be tired, even stressed and looking for some much needed rest, a little peace and quiet. Our partner may have had a difficult time and is looking for some TLC, a little back rub–some form of soothing touch. What often happens instead is an exchange of words expressing irritation, blame and intense dissatisfaction. A strong disagreement and a fight may even follow. The underlying needs and wants never get expressed. This can happen.

It can be helpful to consider the way we make our needs and wants known to each other. This is an action part in our marriage relationship. With patient practice and increasing confidence, we can avoid those skirmishes with each other. Looking to the unmet needs underlying our fights and disagreements can really help us grow in our relationships.

• *What are your unmet needs and wants at this time in your life?*
• *How do these unmet needs affect your marriage relationship?*

Growth takes place one day at a time.

Addressing Our Partner's Needs

Everyone needs and wants affection. For some of us it may be easier to give than to take in affection. There is a little child in all of us wanting affection and our age does not matter. It is not something meant only for kids, and not adults. When we are around children, we seem to recognize their needs and we often express affection easily. We kiss, hug and hold children as if we easily acknowledge their vulnerability and need for such expression of affection.

What about ourselves as adults? Can we read those same needs and wants in each other? If your affection is based on what you receive in return, like sex, you are manipulating your partner.

• How natural do you feel expressing affection to each other?
• How do you make known your needs for attention
and affection?

Growth takes place one day at a time.

Wanting Our Peace And Quiet

When too much sound reaches our ears and our peace and quiet is disturbed, we tend to believe our rights have been violated. Ideally, we want no problems or very few. We like advance warning of all possible harm and disappointment, no difficult decisions to make and no adversarial relationships. This is not our real world.

The above could be achieved but not without paying a price. We would withdraw within ourselves, commit to very little and avoid any deep caring or involvement with others. When we choose to be passionate, caring, involved and committed, we are choosing an active and engaged life with another. We expect ups and downs and we do not become overly troubled when our peace and tranquility is disturbed.

• How peace-filled are you?
• Are you paying a price?
• How are you coping with the disturbances and frustrations
in your life right now?

Growth takes place one day at a time.

Appreciating Each Other's Contribution

We like our work to be appreciated and respected. Maintaining a well-functioning marriage and family requires a collaborative effort. Do you ever take up tasks on the basis of gender or stereotyped roles? We tend to assign status and acceptance to certain tasks. In some instances, subtle and not-so-subtle remarks are made regarding the importance of our different tasks. Intellectual work may claim higher ranking than manual work. Such categorizing can turn out to be simple snobbery.

In marriage, our cooperative effort in taking responsibility for house and children is a vote for equality and cooperation. The difficulty with categorizing is that it becomes very close to defining the importance of each other in limiting and biased ways. We also run the risk of being labeled inferior and superior.

• *Does a work hierarchy exist in your relationship?*
• *What effect does your mutual cooperation have on your ability to live and work as a team?*

Growth takes place one day at a time.

Honor What We Do

As Americans we have a reputation for being practical and action oriented. We often approach our work with the intention of getting it done and moving on. This approach, as effective as it often is, can contain some pitfalls. When we are in a hurry, we run the risk of overlooking some important things along the way. Dedication is praiseworthy but it can often turn into blind obsession.

Integrity and honesty, giving our best to what we do, need not cause an imbalance in our life. We should take pride in what we do. "Take our job and shove it" is a song; it is not an attitude that helps us reach our goals. When honest effort and integrity guide our work, we have balance, a sense of direction and a dedication that gives meaning to what we do. This is a good time to evaluate and ponder what our work means to us. Consider the various aspects of your work and how your attitude influences what you do.

- *What attitude do you bring to your work, wherever you are and whatever you do?*
- *What guides you in your approach to doing your work?*

Growth takes place one day at a time.

Something For Me, Something For Us

It is not an easy task to communicate to our partner when we want something for ourselves and when we want something together. Often when we proclaim something for ourselves we experience our partner hurt, left out, rejected. A decision to attend an evening class can be interpreted by our partner as simply another way of saying we do not want to stay home.

When our communication with each other is good and the relationship is on solid and trusting ground, the issues arising from decisions involving self and together are less complicated. Consider your own relationship and how decisions are made regarding independent choices and together choices. Often problems surface when one is involved in a work activity that requires that person to be away for long periods of time. Discuss this matter with each other and check out the possible application to your relationship.

•How clear is your communication regarding
what you want for yourself?
• How clear is your communication regarding your needs
and wants from your partner?
• In what way are independent choices and together choices
important for your relationship?

Growth takes place one day at a time.

Having Fun Together

In this era of leisure time and activities, we may still find ourselves struggling to have time and fun together. Some of us even work hard at having fun. Interests are not always mutual and discord can occur when we seem unable to choose an activity that interests each at the same time. This calls for understanding, flexibility, compromise and negotiation.

Trade-offs can work and often are a creative way for handling a situation that involves the choice of activities we want to do together. How are you handling your leisure time? Do you even consider it important for yourself and your relationship? Do your interests match? The pendulum swings back and forth for most of us doing alone–doing together. How does this work out for you and your relationship?

- *How are you taking time for yourself?*
- *How do you negotiate spending leisure time together?*
- *What are some of your major obstacles to having fun with each other?*

Growth takes place one day at a time.

A Day To Reminisce

This is a day for memories. There is a freshness in the air and the weather invites us to reflect on shorter days, cool evenings, children beginning school, bands practicing, football practices, buttered sweet corn and red tomatoes. Beginnings and endings coming together.

Are there longings to return in time to what could have, should have, would have been? Has time simply gone by too fast and left you with a short memory or can you look back at school, at the friends you made and left and be grateful for all that has been? This is an opportunity to reminisce and share your thoughts and feelings with each other. Perhaps a walk in a park, a visit to some familiar place, a high school football game, a place to just share.

- *What memories are evoked in you today?*
- *What feelings do you feel as you attempt to make contact with your own personal experiences somewhere in time?*

Growth takes place one day at a time.

The Expert That Is You

This is a great time to be classified as an "expert." We seem to have accepted such a reference as legitimate and praiseworthy. We have "experts" on every corner telling us what constitutes "normality" and "abnormality." An exception is when we run into something that is "not specific." This tells us that the data are not yet all in. The data, however, will probably never be all in. The events and experiences in our life will never fall neatly into some category that will label us "normal" or "abnormal."

Comparing ourselves with others, even with our respected friends and personal idols, will rarely if ever lead us to much. This does not mean we should, therefore, become complacent and totally self-satisfied. We can get into the habit of evaluating and examining our thoughts, feelings and behavior without labeling them and with the intention of wanting to simply learn about ourselves. Let's avoid judging ourselves too harshly. Appreciating our giftedness will go a long way.

> • *How can you become more trusting and believing*
> *in your own giftedness?*
> • *Do you honor and respect each other's contributions to the*
> *marriage?*

Growth takes place one day at a time.

Getting To Know Us Is Special

When someone special notices us, makes eye contact with us, we sense the importance of that person to us and we sense our own importance. It is a very powerful experience to have someone wanting to know us. There is something very special and personal in all of this for us. We in turn want to reach out to them and get to know them better. It develops into a mutuality and that feeds our love in a very special way. Inwardly and kind of secretly, we want and need another to come looking for us.

It is when our partner lets us know that he/she has not yet figured us all out and is wanting to know even more, that we feel our bond together being strengthened. This is a good time to try to go beyond the surface and look for those special qualities that once drew you to each other. Don't be reticent to share what you find.

- *How is your partner special to you?*
- *How special do you feel you are to your partner?*
- *What are some of the things that give you a sense of being special just as you are?*

Growth takes place one day at a time.

The Choices We Are Making

A powerful force in our marriage is the recognition and understanding of the choices we make. Who usually makes them? Is there a reliance upon one person usually or do both get involved in the process? Some of us choose by consensus. It depends upon our ability to gather others around to support us first. This could be our children, friends or relatives.

Do we ever consider our choices as reflective of our marriage and the direction we are headed? We can often see how this applies to us individually but not as a couple. It is well to reflect on the choices we are making both individually and as a couple. Consider any area in your marriage and discuss how choices are made and by whom.

> • *How comfortable are you in making decisions*
> *that affect your life?*
> • *How are decisions made in your marriage relationship?*
> • *What do you like about the way decisions are made*
> *in your relationship?*
> • *What don't you like?*

Growth takes place one day at a time.

What Bugs Me About You

When we take the time to be with each other and identify those areas in the relationship that really "bug" us, we go a long way toward achieving a hopeful sense that we are growing together. Often, it is the identification of one area that allows us to handle the other areas involved.

"What bugs me the most about you." When we can answer this honestly without worrying whether our marriage will survive, then we are on our way to developing honest and open communication with each other. Of course, it takes practice and it does involve some risk since it will involve an invitation to be open and a willingness to learn from each other. All of this is not easy and you need to support each other along the way.

- *What does your partner do that bugs you?*
- *How can honest and open communication help you in your relationship?*
- *What are some of the risks involved?*

Growth takes place one day at a time.

Learning From Old Hurts

We may have married before and we are attempting to be as happy as we can be in this marriage. Have we resolved old attachments? Are there any old feelings lingering on such as sadness, blame or anger? There is a certain emptiness that may linger on. Just as there is a death of anything human, marriages too can die.

There is, however, a new life that can be ours if we truly want to make it occur. We try to admit our contributions to whatever happened in the past. Simplistic labels such as, "oh, he was an alcoholic," or "she had an affair," do not allow us to learn much from those experiences and contribute to our unsettlement and unresolved conflicts within ourselves. Let's pray and work daily to achieve self-knowledge, forgiveness and openness to new life right where we are now.

- *How are you dealing with the hurts in your life?*
- *How have your hurts affected your relationship with your partner?*
- *What is your ability to share your hurts with each other?*

Growth takes place one day at a time.

Sending Our Message Clearly

There is probably no household around that does not have someone shaking his or her head as if to say, "what just happened? I don't understand." Just as unfinished projects can leave clutter around and cause upheaval, so can unfinished messages sent to each other cause confusion, irritation and a lack of closure that often leads to frustration and unnecessary bickering.

Sometimes such disconnection in our communication can lead to serious questioning of self and the marriage. We are not even aware of the incompleteness of our messages and so we can help ourselves by paying attention to the frustration, the confusion, the sudden reactions we give to a message that to us sounds either incomplete or confusing. Checking out with each other what you hear can be very helpful in combating any use of incomplete messages you may be sending to each other.

• How clear and complete is your communication
to your partner?
• How do you check for such clarity and completeness
with each other?
• What could you do to encourage and help each other
communicate clearly?

Growth takes place one day at a time.

Seeing Our Realities Clearly

We want our lives to go smoothly and so we make sacrifices of various kinds so that nothing or very little causes us to be upset. Yet, there are times when a healthy argument, a burst of anger, can clear the air and move a situation along and off center. We find ourselves letting something go and that causes us discomfort simply because no one intended the discomfort to occur in the first place.

Sending clear messages to each other takes practice and determination. Seeing through goodwill and good intentions to the reality of what is going on takes a firm intention not to be deterred or distracted from what is at hand. You cannot build the relationship you want without having occasional struggles that confront each other's "built-in" preconceptions and expectations. Discuss this reality with each other.

• What role does anger play in your relationship?
• Can you recall the last time you were angry with your partner?
• How did you express it? Are you able to vent anger in a healthy manner and move on?

Growth takes place one day at a time.

Listening To Another Point Of View

One of the necessary qualities of good communication that is difficult to learn and practice is a recognition that each of us has our own perspective our own point of view. Someone once said that it is our view from a point—and that point is uniquely our own. It is so very easy to impose our view, our interpretation because it is what comes through our filtering process. It is much more of a challenge to listen so as to understand how another perceives reality.

When we stay around long enough to understand how and what our partner perceives, we will not have to be concerned over how to respond. We will probably experience little need at times to comment. We will experience a sense of well-being and satisfaction and certainly an awareness that our communication is flowing rather easily and without very much effort or strain.

> • *Do you feel your point of view is wanted, appreciated and respected?*
> • *Do you ever feel that you have to "tread on eggs" so as not to say the wrong thing or do you have a comfortable rapport together?*

Growth takes place one day at a time.

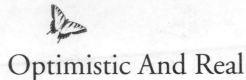

Optimistic And Real

It is quite natural to seek happiness as our goal and to look for signs such as a smile or a voice tone to tell us that everything is well and going fine. The problem is, however, that such criteria, satisfying as they may seem, can also lead us away from our goal and actually serve as subtle distractions and even false evidence posing as the real thing. It is important to check from time to time whether these signals and those signs are for real or whether they have some other purpose. The subtlety can pose as a special gift or some form of new interest that really covers something else. It may be difficult to spot such a thing easily but with effort and a little risk you can open up to each other and talk about it.

- *What are some reasons for you to be optimistic about your relationship?*
- *How realistic and honest can you be with each other?*
- *Can you listen for voice tones as well as words?*

Growth takes place one day at a time.

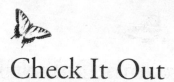

Check It Out

Most of us would not openly tell others what they are thinking or forecast the results of their choices and behavior. In our relationship with our partner, however, we sometimes do just that. This is probably something we do without any malicious intent on our part. It often begins innocently enough with an offer to be helpful and a statement as innocent and as accurate as "you look tired, dear," "you must be angry," "you had a bad day." All may be right on and true.

When these observations are checked out the result can often lead to fruitful communication and a soothing exchange. If not checked for verification with the other, it can often result in misunderstanding, confusion and hurt feelings. Being insightful is one thing, reading another's mind is quite another. The former is helpful and very much needed.

- *What are the ways you check out what you see and hear from your partner?*
- *How can you avoid playing counselor with your partner?*

Growth takes place one day at a time.

Boredom Doesn't Last

A familiar word from teenagers is "Boring." No one, of course, has the corner of the market and all of us, at times, can feel bored. When this happens with us, we have the option of looking for ways to reach out to someone else. It can be an opportunity to look for someone around us who has a need. It may be a simple phone call to make a connection. It may be doing something we have not done for some time. The message is be active, smell the fresh air, get the body active, change your schedule. Of course, we always have the option to simply do nothing and be bored. We can also revel in doing nothing. This can be difficult for some of us who believe we have to be in perpetual motion. Our machinery does not have to be operating at high speed at all times.

- *What are you doing to avoid boredom in your relationship?*
- *How could too much activity and busyness negatively affect your relationship?*
- *What in your relationship contributes most to your relationship?*

Growth takes place one day at a time.

Stop The Hurry Up

It is rather easy to live a surface life. We can touch many things along the way and touch no one thing for long. We can develop a speed that can have us running past others, even our partner, and not recognize what is happening until it is too late. Our marriage becomes a resting place but just long enough so we can get going again. Often our partner, children or friends will try to tell us in different ways that we are not available for them. We can dismiss these warnings easily by reminding them of our good intentions and how they benefit from our hard work.

This is an opportunity to slow down and catch our breath. Pause today to simply feel your body, look around to really see the people you are with and feel what the present moment is for you. Discuss this with your partner and note how this might be occurring in your marriage.

- *How do you try to slow down when everything in you says hurry up?*
- *What are some benefits that could come when you slow down and live more in the present?*

Growth takes place one day at a time.

September 17

Co-Creating Day By Day

Don Williams, in one of his songs, sings of how being with each other is a miracle. It is the freedom that we give to each other to grow in the relationship that continues to enrich our marriage. It is the patience we exercise with each other as we see beyond the everyday happenings to catch little glimpses of each other's personality. The sufferings, the disappointments as well as the joy-filled moments we share, continue to be the things that bind us together.

Daily, we are able to come to know each other better. These are some of the forces that strengthen our commitment to each other and contribute to our realization that we are co-creators in our marriage. Our power to create goes beyond our power to procreate. We create or we die. We look to each other for support and encouragement in all of this.

- *What are some of the experiences that bind you together?*
- *How can you help to continue to create and maintain the marriage you want?*

Growth takes place one day at a time.

Making Ourselves Clear

Some of us have difficulty being direct and assertive. It takes not only the knowledge of how to and the desire to do it, but it also takes a lot of practice and perseverance. We may have gotten used to the reactive, laid-back lifestyle and do not necessarily feel any need to change this. It may be only on occasion when we realize that our lack of directness and lack of clarity has gotten us into situations we no longer can tolerate or want to accept.

Making our thoughts and feelings known is the first step in the direction of a possible solution. Getting into the practice of opening up to others in little ways, safe ways with safe feelings, can often be a good place to start. This will help us when the larger needs occur and it becomes necessary to reveal deeper feelings and needs.

• What are some of the less risky but important feelings, thoughts and needs you could present to your partner today?
• How could your assertiveness help you get your message across clearly to your partner?

Growth takes place one day at a time.

Giving And Receiving

The shopping days immediately following Thanksgiving, Christmas, and Hanukkah are some of the busiest of the year. People are expecting good deals and many are making returns. Many of these returns, I suspect, have something to do with items never really wanted in the first place. We accept gifts we don't particularly like, never asked for, and maybe even said we did not want. There are well-intentioned friends and spouses who give gifts and purchases and pay no attention to the wishes or real needs of the receiver. When these situations occur, it can be helpful as a giver to pay attention to our intention. Is this gift really what he/she wants or needs? As the receiver, we can attempt to direct the giver's generosity in the direction of the real need or want. "Since you are in such a generous mood, and this does not really fit, perhaps we can go shopping together or I could exchange for etc..."

- *When you buy gifts, do you take into consideration your partner's personality, likes and dislikes, and needs?*
- *How can you receive from the generosity of your partner honestly and graciously?*

Growth takes place one day at a time.

Checking Our Family Ties

Family ties are important to most of us. They vary, however, in intensity, importance and meaningfulness. Consider your relationship with father, mother, grandparents, brothers, sisters, uncles, aunts and others. Are they close relationships? Are they distant? With whom are you the closest? Which relationship is most conflictual, most tense?

As you consider your relations today, you may stop along the way and allow yourself to draw upon old memories, whether happy or sad. It is also important to determine whether you maintain your sense of self and speak for yourself or whether you shift over easily to their interests and minimize or even devalue your own. You may need to focus on developing a one-to-one relationship with one of these family members. If so, which one and what will it take to make it happen? Can your partner help in all of this?

- *Which family member are you the closest to? Why?*
- *Which family members are you the most distant with?*
- *What steps are you willing to take to evaluate and strengthen your family ties?*

Growth takes place one day at a time.

September 21

Telling It Out Loud

Like children, we sometimes respond only when someone raises their voice to us. As a recent radio commercial put it, "You can't have an omelet without first breaking the eggs." We sometimes need to be blunt and confront each other about what is happening at a given time in our life and in our relationships. There is a place in every marriage for such confrontations lest we encourage complacency and boredom.

We cannot really develop and nurture a healthy and vibrant relationship without engaging in occasional struggles with each other. We need an occasion to break through some of the myths and unrealistic expectations that we have of each other. The confrontations can and need to leave us standing and not beaten down by verbal abuse, of course. This can be one way to become refreshed as a couple.

• How do you feel about confronting each other?
• How could you make your confrontations with each other a helpful experience for the both of you?

Growth takes place one day at a time.

Owning Our Contributions

One of the most difficult things for many of us to learn to accept is that whatever needs change or correction in our marriage usually involves both of us. It is difficult to always be aware of our own contribution to a conflict or problem. It is, of course, easier and less complicated to blame the other for what is going wrong.

We register our complaints with such introductions as, "If only, if you only, if you would..." These say, in essence, that our behavior is dependent upon what the other does or does not do. We fail to take responsibility for ourselves and the contribution we are making to keep the situation going. If I am the one who is asked to change, it can be helpful to inquire, or at least consider, what will happen to our relationship if I do change. Talk it over. Are "if onlys" operating regularly in your relationship?

- *Can you own your contributions to the problems in your marriage?*
- *How could your honest admission in these areas strengthen your relationship?*

Growth takes place one day at a time.

September 23

Watching The Clues

Sometimes we use our partner's behavior as a cue for our own. This involves a rather subtle resentment and anger that seems to get channeled with a tit-for-tat response. When our partner treats us well, we respond in like manner. When our partner is unthoughtful or acts insensitively, we respond in a similar way. We, therefore, are using each other's behavior as models for our own. Most often, we are not aware of doing this. This calls for a more personal awareness of what our partner is doing, that is in some way triggering certain feelings to be experienced by us. We can begin to separate our feelings from our behavior and take responsibility for our own feelings and how we will respond.

• *Consider how you may be avoiding expressing your true feelings and cuing your responses off of your partner's behavior.*
• *How can understanding your reactions help you with your response to each other?*

Growth takes place one day at a time.

Common Complaints

Complaining can be a futile attempt to make a lot of noise with no intention of making things any different. It can become a common practice in our marriage to notice something we don't like or appreciate and complain about it vigorously. At the time of the occurrence, we may feel a certain nagging frustration and even helplessness. We can, however, get locked into the feeling and the vocal exchanges long after the incident occurs. This suggests that we can easily harbor the feelings and maintain them often without intending to do so.

Dealing with the incident immediately will usually short circuit the process and prevent the ongoing complaining to occur. This calls for an on-the-spot response that lets the other know how we experience the incident and that we will respond accordingly if and when it occurs again. This takes determined practice. This is not an easy one, especially when we are upset. Stay with it.

- *How can your complaints become a helpful resource to your relationship?*
- *When do your complaints contribute negatively to your relationship?*
- *How were complaints dealt with in your home when you were growing up?*

Growth takes place one day at a time.

Indifference As Our Protection

Each of us has our own way of protecting ourselves from real or imagined danger. Since these are uniquely our own, we tend to maintain them long after they are needed. As we grow older we realize, with some effort on our part, that they have served their psychological and emotional purpose. This, however, does not mean we are eager or interested in parting with them. It is only after some painful experiences combined with gentle understanding that we can better control and give up these protections.

Indifference, for example, is not often directly intended. We can tune each other out, through the use of very legitimate means such as our work, tiredness, sleep, even prayer. Our intent is not to allow ourselves to be affected by our partner. Understanding our intentions can lead us to helpful awareness of this particular way of protecting ourselves.

> *• How is indifference expressed in your relationship with each other?*
> *• What is your intention when you use indifference as your protection?*

Growth takes place one day at a time.

Comfort And Support At Our Side

Are there more "wet blankets" in our lifetime than "comforters?" Wet blankets are the ones who spill out gloom and doom messages to us whenever we speak to them of our dreams, our plans and intentions. They are the ones who see reality most of the time in terms of the glass half empty. They anticipate the worst and have a trail of woes to back them up.

Then, there are those who wish us well on our life journey and have words of encouragement and support. Of course, our greatest cheerleader can be our partner. If so, we are truly blest to have our partner at our side cheering us on when we ourselves may not see the reason for any optimism. Check out the ways you support and encourage each other. What works best for one may not necessarily be the best for the other.

- *Identify the ways you support each other and how you experience that support.*
- *Are there any areas in your relationship in which you experience a wet blanket partner instead of a comforting and supportive partner?*

Growth takes place one day at a time.

Making Things Worse

A "neurosis" psychologically involves the ability to make worse that which we seek to enjoy. There is more discomfort and unhappiness in the solution than in the very problem we are trying to resolve. Happiness and joy seem to somehow evade us and we look past those bright areas that may be present but do not allow ourselves to take in. This can often set the stage for catastrophizing and disaster seeking in our marriage.

We need to make it very clear to our worry prone partners that such interpretations of the scene, especially those that have gone on before and turned out satisfactory in the end, will not be allowed to control our relationship and our lives. It is difficult but necessary to check out for accuracy all gloomy predictions and stick to the decisions we know have worked well in the past for us and our relationship.

- *What are some successful strategies you use as a couple to resolve problems in your marriage?*
- *How could a clear assessment of your conflicts and problems contribute to their successful resolution?*

Growth takes place one day at a time.

Crossing Transactions

In the TV program "Crossfire," we expect rebuttal and fast-moving talk and interruptions during the conversations. In our marriage, we expect differently. We expect completed transactions, good listening, uninterrupted complaints. What we often experience, however, are crossed transactions, especially when one attempts to register a complaint

"I wish you would prepare more food rather than small portions." "Well, when was the last time you went shopping with me?" This is a form of blaming and easily hooks the other's anger. Of course you can change the subject to avoid further conflict. It is important that at the time you recognize such cross transactions, you raise your hand to signal "stop." It can be helpful if the one registering the complaint specifically announce the complaint again clearly. The crossed transaction may not be intentional and thus needs to be addressed by both partners. The sooner the better.

* *What is your understanding of crossed transactions?*
* *How could you help each other prevent such transactions from occurring?*
* *What could you personally do when they occur in your relationship with each other?*

Growth takes place one day at a time.

Have A Good Day

Today is a day for rejoicing, for simply deciding that it is a "good day." I really do not have to come up with a lot of reasons for this day to be a "good day." A realization that I am alive, an awareness that the world out there is in perfect order, that I can question life and life can question me.

Today, I can feel strength in the beliefs and convictions I have about things that affect my life. I realize that I am not a pawn in the design of someone else but rather I am special and important to others and I can tell when I am using others and others are using me. Today is a day for pauses and wonderings of appreciation for what I have and what I have tried to make happen that brings peace and joy into my life and those I love and care for.

> • *Spend some time today personally being aware of the goodness in yourself and the goodness around you.*
> • *How are you a blessing to each other?*

Growth takes place one day at a time.

Building More Cohesion

Chaos and disruption occur in families when tasks and responsibilities are not clearly identified and assigned. This may not be regarded as very romantic, but it is crucially important for a workable marriage and a functional family. Part of the satisfaction and security that occurs in our marriage occurs when there are clear agreements as to expectations, authority, responsibilities.

When we accomplish this, we strengthen the unity and security of our relationship. Predictable behavior, carrying out assigned tasks, negotiating differences, nourishes and adds to building cohesion and strengthening our marriage and family. We need to respect the talents of each other and work out ways that we can each contribute. We can discuss those areas where we feel we can best contribute. When these details are handled well, we are left with more time for leisure events and positive energy for other interests and activities.

- *What issues in your relationship trigger chronic disagreement?*
- *Would clarity of responsibilities, expectations, and tasks be of help here?*

Growth takes place one day at a time.

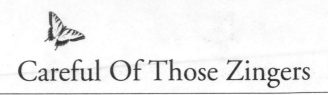

Careful Of Those Zingers

On probably more occasions than we can recall we have been asked, "Can't you take a joke?" "Why are you so thin-skinned?" Usually these are in reference to some kind of ethnic joke or story or even our own family background. These questions or statements are often accompanied by a forced smile or even a form of upset. Of course, when we are on the receiving line of such remarks, we can have difficulty maintaining our own composure and keep from saying something back. Most of us can somehow tell whether it is a remark made innocently or if someone, including our partner, is attempting to express anger and get at us for something. When references to our national or family background are made, we should nip it in the bud. They can easily become zingers for fueling conflicts and leave trails of bitterness, hurt and angry feelings.

- *What are some of the ways your anger leaks out with your partner?*
- *What role does humor play in the expression of your anger?*

Growth takes place one day at a time.

When We Feel Stuck

"We feel stuck." Not an uncommon statement from one in the marriage. It suggests a number of possibilities. One, there is boredom and neither of us knows what to do about enlivening our relationship. It could also be that we are at an impasse and we can't seem to get off center. We may argue and discuss, all to no avail. We get only so far and we throw up our hands in frustration and disappointment. It is at these times that we can discover our need for a new approach.

We can approach each other with the attempt to accept each other's thoughts and feelings and behavior at face value. There is no top dog nor is one more right than the other. There are no good or bad feelings—they just are. We will not censure each other and we acknowledge the possibility of each being of goodwill and committed to becoming unstuck. Now that we can admit the problem, where can we go from here? Take some time with each other to talk about this one.

- *In what areas of your relationship do you experience an impasse?*
- *What could you do to help resolve the impasse?*

Growth takes place one day at a time.

Consider A Checkup

We are living in a time of a wellness revolution. The food menu we choose is a reflection of our sincere determination to join the ranks of the hearty healthy. We have our moments of frustration and successes. We acknowledge that early resolutions can become delayed intentions and we look for shortcuts to success like so many of our friends. Taking care of ourselves is a worthy and necessary pursuit for all of us and as a goal it receives the support of most of us.

Perhaps such zealous efforts that include the annual physical could include an annual marriage checkup. This could be done with or without the help of a professional counselor. The idea may not be far-fetched, especially when we consider the importance of a prevention approach in living our lives. The task need not be complicated nor scary. It can be revealing, but then isn't this sensible for those of us who want to grow and be happy? A visit to the library can be a good beginning. Look in the section on marriage. If no luck, call a marriage counselor.

> • *What are your views and feelings regarding*
> *a marital checkup?*
> • *How could such a checkup assist you in your efforts to keep*
> *your marriage alive and growing?*

Growth takes place one day at a time.

Responding Together

When we think of how complex marriage can be, we wonder how any of us can survive the many conflicts and changes. There is no marriage without some form of conflict or discord. It is possible, and even probable, that many of us will not only survive, but even grow and achieve workable and satisfying relationships.

There are always, of course, circumstances that will occur in our lives requiring our responses. In this way, we are involved in change. It may be a new job, a new baby, a friendship, a disaster or unexpected trial we must face. Much has to do with how we deal with and manage change in our lives. When so much is happening, we realize that it takes courage and much patience to remain involved and committed. We may even conclude that our marriage is really better than we sometimes think.

* *Is there some situation or circumstance needing your mutual response?*
* *What can you do to encourage your partner's cooperation and effort?*
* *How does a strong sense of mutuality, of togetherness, strengthen your commitment and security with each other?*

Growth takes place one day at a time.

Sharing Our Talents

It seems a lot easier to issue tasks to our partner than to acknowledge our own talents and interests. A most invigorating process is to be able to consider where our talents lie and to accept trade off tasks. This can prevent unnecessary struggles and we can use our energy more constructively with each other. This can involve working at a task side by side, even when we seem dissimilar.

When we agree on what particular tasks and duties each will assume, we reduce the possibility of running into each other over the same task or interfering with each other's performance. The decisions as to who will do what, even if it comes to who will plan the weekend activities, can contribute to a mutual sharing process. With practice and steady successes, we can learn to trust and respect each other's contribution to making the marriage a mutual sharing of tasks and responsibilities.

- *How can you use your individual talents to benefit your relationship?*
- *What current obstacles stand in the way of the use of your talents?*
- *How could you help each other in this matter?*

Growth takes place one day at a time.

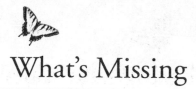

What's Missing

We have our own perceptions and beliefs about specific things in our life. In other words we see "it," whatever "it" is, always in the same way. The words "if only" are most often used in reference to something that isn't present, although we would like it to be. Its use is interpreted by us as a cause or at least a contributing reason why we cannot or did not achieve something. There is, however, another way of interpreting "if only," and that is in a more positive and creative way. We can consider as many different pictures, scenes, happenings as we are able to come up with. These are the different ways that we can sharpen our creative imagination. Think of as many different "if onlys" you can come up with regarding your marriage. Do this without considering the logicalness or the sensibility of it all. This can appeal to the creative part in you. It can be fun and possibly open up some new doors for you. Have fun with this one.

- *What creative pictures, thoughts come to mind when you consider "if only" and apply it to your marriage relationship?*
- *How could such strengthening of your imagination be of benefit?*

Growth takes place one day at a time.

Negotiating Our Needs And Wants

It is not uncommon to feel a sense of futility in our efforts to experience harmony and a smooth give-and-take in our marriage. We become aware, often with a shudder, that perfect harmony is rare, if not impossible, and that we have to learn specific ways to handle specific needs in our marriage.

I am referring to the ever necessary and important task of negotiating our needs and wants. For some of us, this may seem an awkward and unnecessary task, but one nevertheless that can make the difference between a successful or unsuccessful relationship. We may be of the mind that such activity is meant for the bargaining table at work. Some of us maintain that we should always bend our wills to serve the other and always be ready to give in for the sake of peace and harmony. This may bring about a short-lived peace and lead to short-lived arguments, but could fuel resentment and an imbalance that could jeopardize our relationships. This is worth some discussion time.

- *How do you negotiate your needs and wants with each other?*
- *What success are you having?*
- *What help can you offer each other in this process?*

Growth takes place one day at a time.

A Follow Up On Yesterday

To follow up on yesterday's thoughts, an added consideration is in order. We may realize that this very important task of negotiating with each other is difficult and we may need help to learn the process. That is fine. Such a desire to learn can be of immense help because our goodwill and sincere intentions are present.

We can also become aware that holding up someone else's relationship as a model and what is happening to them can be a very non-convincing argument with our partner. We all want to be recognized as capable and able in our own right. When our differences are so deep and we feel so far apart as to accentuate a sort of digging in by one of us, it is still possible for one of us to honestly concede that area or issue to the other and move on.

- *What skills do you use in negotiating your needs and wants with each other?*
- *What new skills would you like to acquire?*
- *What help is available in order for you to acquire and develop these skills?*

Growth takes place one day at a time.

Our Judgment Calls

Sports umpires frequently have to make judgment calls. "They calls them as they sees them" is an old reference to what they do. We also see things daily in our lives and make judgment calls. Our values, beliefs and feelings all click in as we make our observations that sometimes come out as judgments. This is a process that occurs instantly and we do not even realize our sudden assessment of the situation until we have our say.

This is one feature in our marriage that can use frequent monitoring because it is so easy to find ourselves sitting on the judgment seat. Is it not possible that after we observe another's action and how it differs from what we would do, we could give ourselves just a little more time before responding? Attempting to understand what we see and hear allows us an opportunity to make life a lot easier for everyone.

- *Are you making too many judgment calls and not enough listening calls?*
- *What can you do to avoid making judgments?*
- *How would such an effort benefit your relationship?*

Growth takes place one day at a time.

The Unexpected

Many of us like when our lives, our work, our marriage, our relationships in general go smoothly and there is a kind of tranquility that exists for us. We are not likely to take to confusing circumstances, situations that occur unplanned, and people popping in uninvited. We are apt to want to put people and things "in their place," so we can get back to "normal."

Consider for a moment, however, that when upheaval and a kind of dissonance occurs in our lives, we take the time and produce the energy to look for creative solutions. It is almost as if those problems, those conflicts, those areas of upheaval call for us to respond in ways we otherwise would not respond. We can become strengthened as individuals and as couples when we face and deal with these occurrences in our lives.

- *How important is it to be in control of circumstances and the flow of events in your life?*
- *What unexpected results occur when you allow your creativity to respond to the unexpected in your personal life and in your marriage?*

Growth takes place one day at a time.

Check Out Our Assumptions

An assumption is like a coin having two different sides. On the one side, our assumption can lead to further exploration and discovery. On the other hand, it can contain elements that may lead us to form wrong conclusions and promote complications that need careful exploration and gentle confrontation. Often, what we believe and perceive at a given moment may not be what is occurring at all.

It can be helpful to consider the assumptions we make about each other, others and our world in general. Our prejudices, biases, misunderstandings, often enter into our lives with greater frequency than we know or care to admit. They discolor our conversations and can cause mistrust to enter our relationships. Check with yourself and your partner how assumptions play a role in your marriage and family. You may want to include the world scene, or any other scene.

- *What do you assume about your partner?*
- *What does your partner assume about you?*
- *What role does assumption play in your relationship?*

Growth takes place one day at a time.

Acknowledging Each Other

One of the common courtesies we appreciate is when we experience ourselves being acknowledged by those around us. Problems easily occur when we fall short of letting each other know that we have really heard what they have said to us. If children are at home, we probably have had the experience of short cuts in our communications with each other. A check on the way we talk to each other as well as how we complete our conversations could be helpful today.

Consider what happens at the table when someone asks for something to be passed. Are names used, are direct requests made, are "thank yous" used as acknowledgements, are grunts and groans used as substitutes for clear verbal expression? All of us can gain by exploring this one since these occurrences are common in every marriage and family. Clear and direct communications are positive ways to connect with each other.

- *Are there instances when you do not feel acknowledged by your partner?*
- *How do you respect and acknowledge each other's presence?*

Growth takes place one day at a time.

Observing And Learning

Much of what happens around us and inside of us goes unnoticed and undetected. It does not necessarily imply we don't care. It takes a willingness on our part and some practice to recognize, identify and share what we observe in ourselves and especially in each other. As we become good at this sort of thing, we strengthen our relationships and make it possible for meaningful communication to occur. Of course, when we agree to share these observations with each other, it can be most helpful to begin first with the most innocent and easy to observe signs we see. "When you tug on your earlobe and start to laugh I know you want to be close to me." Spend some time together and share these with each other. Have fun learning about each other.

- *Can you think of some behaviors, expressions of your partner that send specific messages to you?*
- *Can you share what you are learning from each other?*

Growth takes place one day at a time.

Including Others

Our society encourages rugged individualism and praises personal effort and success. This, of course, can foster personal growth and achievement and appeals to "the American way." We need, however, to balance this with our involvement and participation with others in community. This may be our church, synagogue, local area or interest group. We need others. When God created us He made the point that it is not good for us to be alone.

There is a much broader application of those words than a simple reference to one's partner. We gain something special when we become involved in a sharing process with another. We can feel a sense of union, of support, of identification and know that we are not alone. This can be very powerful and enriching for us as individuals and as couples. Consider your involvement and participation in community. Talk it over. Get involved.

• How much do you need others in your life?
• How much, as a couple, do you need other couples in your life?
• What can you do today to extend yourself to someone other than your partner?

Growth takes place one day at a time.

Staying On Target

Just as it is easy to bring in side issues to reinforce our point of view in an argument, so we can make references to past behavior to reinforce our views with each other. "You are late, like you were yesterday." Recalling past behavior and relating it to a current situation, even when it resembles the present situation, is just pouring more hot coals on the fires of our conflicts.

Remaining in the here and now, with the current situation as it occurs takes discipline, goodwill and a lot of practice. As we get good at doing so, we increase self-respect and the respect we have for each other. We also direct our energies in a specific direction as well as avoiding the risk of escalating the conflict. Talk to each other about this and note if either of you slip into this heat and no light producing method.

- *How difficult is it to remain focused when you are in a heated argument?*
- *What are some ways you can help each other remain focused during times of disagreement?*

Growth takes place one day at a time.

Nurturing Our Gifts

It is well known by most of us that it can be so easy to pick the fleck of dirt out of the pepper, the tiny flaw out of a seemingly otherwise perfect pattern, etc. We can develop the habit so well we don't even know we are doing it. If we do it to others we undoubtedly learned to do it to ourselves first.

Even the gifts we possess in terms of talent may not only go unseen and unrecognized but we may even prefer to recognize only the "big ones." The gift of being able to stand up and talk to a large audience, of course, would be so much "bigger" than simply doing an act of kindness to a neighbor. We tend to compare our talents with others, thus relegating our own gifts to a less desirable place of importance. When we can truly appreciate our own gifts, no matter how small they may seem, we will become better able to appreciate our partner's gifts.

• Do you really appreciate your gifts?
• Do you allow yourself to recognize them without hearing the word "selfish" somewhere in the background?
• How are you appreciating each other's gifts and talents?
• How are you nurturing those gifts in each other?

Growth takes place one day at a time.

Looking For Answers

At times, it is difficult not to be pessimistic, disillusioned and bitter. It may seem that there exists no bright news at all. We question everything—even our hopes. We tend to question our decisions, even our decisions of faithfulness, when we seem to feel like we are running out of steam and our life takes on a sameness with a dreary monotony.

When our experience tells us we need some sort of help, then we need to listen and try to sort out what is needing attention. It may simply be ourselves, and our need is to share this with our partner and/or close friend. It is "hang in there" power, supported by our own trust and belief in ourselves and in our God that can slowly and ever so gently, nurture and nourish our hope. Today is a wonderful opportunity to look at this one.

*• Are there times when you second-guess yourself
and your marriage?*
• What is most helpful to you when these occur in your life?
• How could your partner be of help in those instances?

Growth takes place one day at a time.

Uncovering Our Potential

Most of us at some time have pondered the direction of our lives and our marriage. Is our vision of what we really want for our marriage relationship still intact or has it drastically changed? We attempt to live the circumstances of our lives daily and only on occasion do we ever consult our vision. It can be revealing and helpful to consider how we are living out the vision we once had.

We grow in our relationship to the degree we are living out our vision of the relationship we not only once had, but of the relationship we now want. Looking at what we want our relationship to be is always helped by considering what it is we really have right now. The difference between what we want and can envision and what we truly have right now is a way of telling us that we are moving in a creative and positive direction. The difference between the two is our potential yet to be experienced. This is a practical and simple way for discovering where we are in our marriage.

- *Are you aware of your potential to become all that you can be?*
- *How can you continue to discover your potential for greater happiness and satisfaction in your marriage?*

Growth takes place one day at a time.

A Preventive Approach

General maintenance of my cars is now a habit with me. At one time I needed to take them in for service when something went wrong with them. This is probably true of our marriage relationships. We consider reaching out for help when our problems become so acute that we seriously consider separation.

The idea of a preventive checkup is not new. It is, however, an idea that is used only in a very limited way. Often we tend to deny that our relationships are worsening. Our marriages deserve the same preventive attention as anything else we have and that we want to preserve. An annual checkup is being used more and more to evaluate our assets as well as our liabilities and identify those natural change areas that accompany any living entity such as a marriage. There is mounting evidence that a competent third party can exert a very positive influence. Just another reminder of what we considered earlier. Time for a checkup.

- *How serious are you about keeping your marriage relationship alive and vibrant?*
- *What efforts are you making to support your good intentions?*
- *What prevention efforts appeal to you?*

Growth takes place one day at a time.

Loving Ourselves

We have heard it said and it may be hard for some of us to believe, "I cannot love another if I do not truly love myself." The idea of loving ourselves, for some of us, may be identified with having a big ego, lack of humility and self-centeredness. Loving ourselves is not a case of being absorbed in ourselves.

I can begin to acknowledge what I think, feel, and want, and value these as necessary in order to function as a healthy, productive human person. My partner can benefit immensely from my honest and accurate evaluation of myself. It serves as an invitation for him or her to acknowledge his or her own true value. Feeling good about ourselves strengthens and energizes our marriage. Remember, God said for us to love others as much as we love ourselves. Not more, not less, but certainly as much.

• Are you comfortable loving yourself?
• Does your relationship support such a belief?
If so, how? If not, why not?
• How do you love yourself?

Growth takes place one day at a time.

Patiently Working Together

"Beware of the devil bearing gifts," a statement I heard when I was growing up. We seem to have an innate distrust and suspicion of anyone promising quick and easy solutions to problems. This approach has probably saved us from some form of calamity or unnecessary grief. Short-term gain often leads to long-term pain.

A careful and organized approach to issues and concerns in our relationships and family matters provides for restful nights down the road. Recognizing and paying attention to the way we work together on our problems and concerns can provide some valuable insights into our relationship. Patience is an important part of our problem-solving strategy. We may have to allow for large doses of patience with situations and with each other in order to bypass the quicker and simpler but less effective approach. Be patient, it helps.

- *How patient are you with yourself?*
- *How patient are you with each other?*
- *What area in your life, your marriage, is requiring your patience?*

Growth takes place one day at a time.

Looking Back

We seem to have an uncanny ability to seek out the negative. We tend to overlook the positive in our lives and instead pick out the failures, the disappointments, the unhappy times.

The past comes alive for us in different ways. It can be a picture of some happy event in our lives together hanging on a wall. A momento we saved that now lies in full view on a shelf in the living room may remind us of a pleasant past experience. We may visit a place where we once experienced something special. The efforts we make to remind ourselves and each other of the happy and special moments in our lives can have a very positive influence on us. Look around in your memories and identify some of those pleasurable moments.

• What are some of the ways you can help to recall those events?
• Share those memories and consider ways you could revive those moments that are so meaningful to you and your partner.

Growth takes place one day at a time.

October 23

Total Care

Paying attention to our body is essential for our self-esteem and is not the same as self-preoccupation. It is important to accept ALL of me and not accept exceptions. Eating the right food is as important as getting adequate exercise. Brushing our teeth regularly is as important as paying attention to our feet. Knowing and experiencing our sexual and sensual feelings is a major way of taking care of ourselves and contributing to our self-esteem. The clothes we wear, the amount of makeup used, the care of our hair, the way we walk, all can be considered in the light of our efforts to care about ourselves realistically. Denying the importance of our body and favoring or accentuating the importance of our intellectual self can isolate a natural part of ourselves.

*• Consider your acceptances of your body and
how you care for your physical needs.*
• How can you help each other stay in good physical shape?
• How could the establishment of a daily routine be of help?

Growth takes place one day at a time.

Staying In Touch

Frequently, we hear references to the "good old days." Often, these are the days prior to marriage. We seemed much more sensitive to the needs of each other and that was fine. We took the time to anticipate what the other might want and it seemed no great shakes to go out of our way to be helpful. One of the noticeable traits in our relationship then was our attention to each other.

How are you doing in this department now? Have you stopped doing things for each other? This seems to be one of the first things to go. We do not know the reasons at all times, but when tension and doubts spring up in our relationship, one of our concerns we can look to is whether we still do things for each other. A renewal of effort in this direction could go a long way to revitalize the relationship.

- *What little things do you like to do for your partner?*
- *What little things do you like your partner to do for you?*

Growth takes place one day at a time.

Experiencing Our Power

Seldom do we consider power as one of the basic needs for having a successful relationship. Power is the experience we feel when we know that when we speak someone is truly listening. We need to know that we are being taken seriously. We run the risk of experiencing ourselves discounted and our power as a person, reduced. When this happens, we are in need of getting that power back. This does not mean it was taken away by someone. It could mean that we decided to place it in storage, hold back. Regaining that power may take time and practice.

It may also be situational and occurring only with certain people in our life. It is important to identify those situations, circumstances and people. Consider the meaning that power has for you and the ways you express it in your relationship as well as the obstacles to the use of that power. This is important and needs your attention and honest sharing.

- *How is power experienced and expressed in your marriage relationship?*
- *What can you do to maintain your power?*
- *Are you being taken seriously?*

Growth takes place one day at a time.

Feeling Validated

Having conflict and problems is a given in every relationship. No exceptions. When these occur, we attempt to deal with them as constructively and positively as we can.

One of the first steps and a very powerful one is to validate the claims of our partner. In this way, we are sending the message that what he or she experienced is real and important. He or she is being taken seriously. In many instances, it takes a bite out of the conflict. It is our attempt to say, "I am trying to understand what it is like for you to be where you are now." This is no simple task and we can often fail in our efforts. It is, however, a welcomed gift we give to each other. We all need the assurance that what we feel is real. We are affirming each other when we validate each other's experience. You may need to discuss it later. The validation is truly a giant first step.

- *How do you feel validated in your relationship?*
- *What can you do to validate each other?*
- *What are some obstacles to feeling validated in your marriage?*

Growth takes place one day at a time.

Voice Quality

Unless we are auditioning for a singing part in a play or choir, we probably do not pay much attention to the sound of our voice. This marvelous instrument is a reminder of how wonderfully we are made. Some spend long hours training their voices to resonate and express an ideal form of sound.

Some of us pay no attention to the sound of our voice. We listen to the voices of others and we experience different reactions. Some voices we hear beckon us to listen because they are soft and gentle. Some voices are strong and assertive. Some are harsh and shrill and put us at a distance or in a state of caution.

What of your voice? Are you aware of the quality of your voice? Ask a true friend to tell you how you sound. Record your voice and listen to its sound. With sensitivity and practice, our voices can speak wonders for us. Share your discovery with your partner.

- *What is the quality of your voice?*
- *What importance does the sound of your partner's voice have for you?*
- *How does your voice enhance or detract from the effectiveness of your communication?*

Growth takes place one day at a time.

Balanced Attention

Loving and respecting our emotions is an essential way of loving ourselves. This helps us maintain our positive self-esteem. We can do this through positive mind talk that encourages and nurtures us. These self-loving messages are important for our growth.

It is also important to receive nurturing from our partner, but if we do not have a positive self-love, then we turn to another to fill the void. This will not be sufficient. Some of us deny the importance of our feelings. This only contributes to other problems, such as depression, irritability and distancing. Our marriage relationship can become strained when there is not a balance between what we have ourselves and what we expect and need from our partner. Does this balance exist in your relationship?

- *What self messages help you feel good about yourself?*
- *How important is it for you to monitor and take charge of your self talk?*
- *How is it important to talk positive good sense to yourself?*

Growth takes place one day at a time.

Being Clear

We enrich ourselves and the people we live with when we are clear thinkers. Situations arise daily that require some kind of assessment or response from us. Our ability to consider these situations as clearly as we can contributes immensely to our self-esteem and enhances the quality of our relationships.

Some relationships dry up simply because there is no exchange of thoughts and ideas. This can place severe limits on any growth in our relationships and short circuit the ongoing discoveries we need with each other. Consider how you are personally growing in your ability to think clearly. What can you and your partner do to improve or enhance this quality in your relationship? This does not suggest a hurried trip to the library or a quick registration for a class. Consider how you can add to your mental and verbal skills. It could help maintain a vitality and freshness in your relationship.

•Do you value your ability to assess, evaluate and share your ideas with each other?
• Do you respect and appreciate each other's thoughts and do you make time to improve your mental and verbal abilities?

Growth takes place one day at a time.

A Question Of Values

Our decisions reflect our values. When we agree or disagree on the way we spend money, our differences often reflect what we value. Another area is what we do with our time. Of course, our preferences and interests come into play, but under these are often the values we hold. Are we even aware of what our values are? What place do our values have in the way we lead our lives?

Is this an area we ever discuss with our partner? Making a list of our top value items and those representing lower values for us can open our eyes to the significance and importance of various areas in our relationship. We tend to go with what we value the most. Teenagers are not the only ones who feel the pressure of our times. We need to become aware of how our own values as adults can be the target for the pressures coming from our own culture. Discuss these pressures with your partner and how you may be affected personally and as a couple.

- *What are some of the strongest influences on your values at this time?*
- *What values do you hold in common with your partner?*

Growth takes place one day at a time.

Keeping Our Vision Clear

Each of us is a storybook of pilgrims on a journey. We become preoccupied on our journey with a lot of details. This is natural of course, but the larger visions of our life, the larger pictures, tend to become blurred and even non-existent.

Our commitment to our values, to our goals, to the more substantial meanings in our lives, tends to diminish or even lose its appeal. This is why most of us can benefit from a retreat or some time away with each other. We need to step aside and revitalize our values and strengthen our commitments. When was the last time you did something specific to enrich and enhance your marriage relationship? Consider the time and effort you give to other interests. Discuss what you and your partner are doing, or are willing to do to enhance and enrich your marriage.

• Do you essentially agree on the vision for your marriage?
• In what directions are you and your partner taking your marriage in light of your marriage vision?
• Has your marriage vision changed since marriage?
If so, how? If not, why not?

Growth takes place one day at a time.

Lots Of Tender Loving Care

I am amazed, especially during the summertime, what care we give to our lawns and gardens, by the amount of time, money and effort we give to our landscapes. I couldn't help but make a connection with our marriage relationships. I think we mean well and taking or not taking care of our property is meant only as a starting point for reflection. We really can find ourselves busy with legitimate tasks and forget each other.

Our marriage is not meant to be left to run on its own like a kind of electronic device. It needs, like a garden, some tender loving care and regular attention. We have to work out the details on our own. God gave us the talent and the know how, but we have to find ways to put it to use. Usually, our inattention is not some planned scheme. It is often simply a bad habit we get into and a conscious effort can be made to check it out and correct it. Today is simply another time to check it out.

- *How are you feeling nurtured in your marriage?*
- *What are you doing to nurture your partner?*
- *What is your marriage asking of you right now?*

Growth takes place one day at a time.

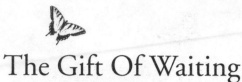

The Gift Of Waiting

What brings you joy? What gives you hope? These are not questions we can quickly answer. Most of us need to know how to wait. Our culture seems to insist on ready answers and solutions to everything. We live in hurry-up times. Waiting can be difficult because it often signals doubts, insecurity and sometimes lack of trust. Solutions and rewards for our efforts are not always just around the corner.

Learning to wait with guarded anticipation for the future takes practice and discipline. It also involves an attitude and a particular approach to the happenings in our life. Consider your plans, your aspirations and hopes for yourself and your marriage. This could be the hidden power in your life and in your marriage. Certain things cannot be rushed. Learn to wait.

- *Is there a waiting and a hopeful perseverance present in your life?*
- *How could such a gift of waiting be given to each other?*
- *What are you waiting for!*

Growth takes place one day at a time.

True Contrition

One of the reasons change may not be occurring in our lives is due to a lack of contrition. We want to move on and we do not want to let go of old habits, old hurts, old memories that continue to have their way. Recognizing and admitting our "not OKness" is as important as admitting our "OKness." We're not always OK!

There are things we still do and say that need to be recognized, admitted and felt bad about, because they are still with us and they need to be confronted and forgiven so we can experience healing. Acting OK needs to be supported by a true interior experience of OKness, otherwise, it is but a coated shell. Loving ourselves is dependent upon a true and honest assessment of the way we truly are. Loving recognizes the shadow in us and goes on. True contrition is essential to loving ourselves and each other.

> • *What needs to be forgiven and let go in your life?*
> • *What needs to be forgiven and let go in your marriage relationship?*

Growth takes place one day at a time.

November 4

Compliments Are Powerful

We may be in a relationship in which compliments and positive feedback are rare and long in coming. This may cause us much sorrow and emptiness. We may, at times, resort to nagging, become critical and even demanding and threatening. Backing off from such efforts and considering other avenues of approach could be more rewarding.

We can remind our partner that his or her specific action or behavior toward us really pleased us and enabled us to feel closer to them. We can then tell them how we would like to experience those same things again. In most instances, this is experienced as neither threatening nor demanding. Let's not let a day go by without looking for and uttering at least one compliment to our partner. When this happens with regularity, our disagreements will most likely be perceived as having less weight and easier to accept and worked with.

- *Do you compliment your partner sincerely every day?*
- *How do you feel when you give compliments? When you receive compliments?*

Growth takes place one day at a time.

Look For The Truth

Humility is truth, to oneself and others. This requires a lot of honesty with ourselves. It means we are open to the truth. This is really what Jesus meant when he said that we need to be meek. If we are, we will be happy and as a bonus, we will inherit the earth. Something to think about. It all reflects a belief that we can walk this earth as eager learners of the truth. It also means that we can acknowledge to ourselves and others that we do not have the market on the truth. We can let go of the opinions and conclusions we formed many years ago. They are not written in stone. We become more flexible, less rigid and authoritative.

Do we pass judgment on ourselves and our partner even before all the data is in? Are we quick to assume guilt and not innocence? Can we look for the good behind our partner's criticism? This is difficult, of course. Look for the kernels of truth. It can help your relationship grow.

- *Can you assume the truth from your partner?*
- *What benefit could such an assumption have for your relationship?*

Growth takes place one day at a time.

Wearing Our Attitude

"Your attitude is showing." We might not often think of that, but it is true. Our attitude is the way we look at people and things in our mind. It goes much beyond our eyesight. The way we look can be negative or positive, but never both at the same time. However, we may be in neither very long.

Ideally, we want to have a positive attitude. The people around us, especially our partner, may not always see us wearing our attitude on our face, but they sense it. Smiling, itself, does not necessarily mean our attitude is positive. It may be masking a hurt, and anger or disappointment. When the outside matches the inside and that inside is OK with the world around us, our smile will be truthful. We want to be more aware that our attitude does show. This could make for a friendly discussion with your partner.

- *What attitude is the easiest to notice in your partner?*
- *What attitude is the easiest for your partner to notice in you?*

Growth takes place one day at a time.

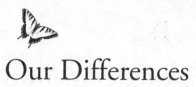

Our Differences

Living with a partner who is very different from ourselves can be tedious, frustrating and wearisome. They are not like us. They are opposites. They think, feel and act differently than we do. We want to change them to become more like us or we want to avoid them when these differences become more pronounced. We feel the impact of that separation between us. We may attempt to discuss these differences openly in order to better understand each other. This takes time and effort.

We can evaluate and attempt to deal with our own thoughts and feelings, and attempt to gain a better understanding of what we are about. Are we rigid in our position on things? Are our differences severe or minor? Do they get to our deeper values or are they more surface areas? Identify and discuss the differences you experience with each other. Look toward understanding the impact of these differences on your relationship.

- *How are your differences manifested in your relationship?*
- *How do these differences affect the way you get along with each other?*

Growth takes place one day at a time.

Honest Admissions

It seems so obvious and simple to just tell it as it is. Be up front, straightforward and honest and the situation will take care of itself. Right? Well, it's not quite that simple. Most of us have learned or heard that aggression, anger and conflict are things to stay away from. Nice people do not raise their voices in anger or discontent. Do we avoid each other when we are angry? Is confrontation scary? How do you avoid it?

Many of our efforts to avoid confrontation are usually temporary efforts to find a solution without hurting our partner. We fail to realize that by protecting ourselves and each other we run the risk of suffocating the relationship. Look for some of the specific ways you avoid confrontation. Silence, hiding behind the newspaper, changing the subject and falling asleep are just some possibilities to start with.

- *How could confrontation become a positive learning experience for you and your partner?*
- *What are some known obstacles to such a positive experience in your marriage?*

Growth takes place one day at a time.

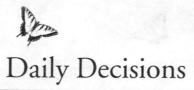

Daily Decisions

A truth is well worth repeating. That is, love must be nourished. Our marriage requires our attention, dedication, commitment and hard work. The effort we put into our relationship brings us good returns. Of course, it must be a mutual effort. Here, women it seems, are first to acknowledge the truth of this. Further, it seems that such effort may take on a sort of personal challenge to be a happier or more productive person. Men, on the other hand, seem to want to contribute to the success and harmony of the relationship, but often question their personal skills to help make it happen.

Loving involves respect, friendship, companionship, communication, passion, nurturing, support and cooperation. These can be cultivated and nurtured by both partners with daily decisions to love and be loved. Trust in your mutual commitment to those daily decisions.

> • *How could your positive daily intentions help*
> *your relationship grow?*
> • *How are your views about loving and growing in agreement?*
> *How do they differ?*

Growth takes place one day at a time.

The Benefit Fits Us

"What's in it for me?" is a familiar question. We seldom, if ever, say this out loud to each other. Perhaps it comes out more as an attack, or an insensitivity toward the other. This is different from compromise or negotiations where we want to give something in order to receive something. Those are legitimate trade offs.

Ask yourself if your attitude toward each other invites compromises, negotiations, and a willingness to talk about your needs openly. Discuss how situations that come up affect both of you. What's in it for us—not just me.

- *Specify your individual needs and the needs you have in common at this time.*
- *How are trade offs used in your relationship?*
- *What are your personally doing that benefits your relationship?*

Growth takes place one day at a time.

Needing And Wanting

It is a true gift, living in today's society, to be able to discern what we need and what we want. There seem to be forces coming from outside as well as inside that pull us in different directions. We face the usual dilemma of living within the budget, disciplining our appetites for this and that.

Can we face the challenges of our needs first, and then consider our wants? How do you, as an individual, fare in this matter? How do you, as a couple, fare in this matter? Talk to each other about your needs and your wants, and how they are affecting your choices and your values.

- *What ways do you have for discerning your needs and wants?*
- *How can you help each other in this process of discernment?*

Growth takes place one day at a time.

Saying We Are Sorry

"Love means never having to say you are sorry." Words from a movie, but also words that could mean that we never experience the power and the care of loving forgiveness. Can we forgive? Can we ask for forgiveness?

The power involved in the act of forgiveness opens us up to new experiences of love and intimacy. It breaks down the obstacles, hindrances and barriers that stand in the way of the openness and caring we need to give and receive from each other.

•*Discuss your ability to forgive and any reservations, as well as the successes, you experience with each other.*

Growth takes place one day at a time.

Looking For The Mystery

"Will you ever learn?" How many of us have heard that one before? One of the worthy goals for us is to strive to keep on learning. To live our lives as learners—open to all that is going on within us and outside of us.

Are we striving to learn about our partner? Can we try to grasp some of the mystery that is him or her? Do we think we have that person all figured out, after all, we have been married to that person for some years now? That would be a serious mistake because when we attempt to make a sure thing out of someone, we run the risk of losing that person. Be open to the mystery in each other. Look for it, and you will find it revealing itself to you each moment of the day in so many different ways. It is a sure cure for boredom.

- *What are some ways you take each other for granted?*
- *What are some of the best ways you learn new things about your partner?*

Growth takes place one day at a time.

Expressing Our Gratitude

What ever happened to thankfulness and gratitude? Do we experience these in our relationship? Do we take time to say "thank you"? When we do, we experience benefit as the giver as well as contribute to the well-being of the receiver. It is a gift we can give to each other, to express gratitude, to say thanks in different ways. Saying thanks can be done in words and perhaps in some form of appreciation.

Gratefulness needs to be expressed. By assuming that our partner knows our good intentions without our having to express them, we risk misunderstanding and losing a precious opportunity. Look and recognize the moments of grace and healing amidst your daily problems, and do yourself a favor by expressing gratitude to each other today.

- *How do you express gratitude to each other?*
- *How is gratitude received and accepted?*

Growth takes place one day at a time.

Clarifying Expectations

Just what are your expectations? Not a bad question to ask when we are feeling the need for a direct clarification on some important matter. Are our expectations of each other clear and expressed directly?

From time to time, it may help to verbalize them and not run the risk of fostering mind reading and promoting misunderstanding. Are there some specific areas in your relationship that are calling for clarification? Check it out for yourself first and then take the time to share it with each other.

- *What expectations did you bring to your marriage?*
- *What expectations do you have of your partner?*
- *In what way could clarifying expectation help your relationship?*
- *How could the expression of your expectations help your relationship?*

Growth takes place one day at a time.

The Direction We Choose

Bishop Fulton Sheen once said, "People rise in the morning and say, 'Good morning, God,' and others say, 'Good God, morning.'" What or who directs our day? Do we line up with the first or the second? How do we motivate ourselves to face our day with its demands, its contacts with others, responsibilities and situations planned and unplanned? Is there time and energy left over at the day's end for each other? Do we view the world in terms of how the world is treating us, or do we take responsibility for our place in the world by deciding how we are going to treat the world around us?

- *Are you treating the world or is the world treating you?*
- *How does your view of your world affect the way you live your day?*
- *How does your decision effect your relationship with your partner and others you live with?*

Growth takes place one day at a time.

Calm Perseverance

Sometimes we arrive at moments in life when we need to simply persevere–to hold steady for awhile. This is not a step backward for us. It is simply a moment, an hour, a day in time to recognize that in our particular situation, we have done all we can do. Now is the time to hold steady–to persevere.

This is not a passive stance or one that suggests we are giving up. It is recognizing the need to simply stand by our mate–to hold steady to our commitment–to pause for another breath. We recognize the need for a calm perseverance that can lead to further grace-filled opportunities and perhaps further action. Ask your partner to discuss with you those times when this happens in your life and in your relationship.

- *What were some times when you simply needed to calmly persevere?*
- *How have these been occasions for learning about yourself and each other?*

Growth takes place one day at a time.

Couple Potential

Growing as a person is understandable, but growing as a couple frequently elicits a blank stare from some of us. Einstein allegedly stated that most individuals use less than 10% of their intellectual potential. Another said that most couples use less than 15% of their potential for growth. Understanding and identifying our potential for growth as a couple is challenging and rewarding.

Do we believe we have already arrived, or are we still open to growing and discovering each other? Do we have each other figured out, or is there still some belief operating in us that our partner will continue to be a mystery never to be fully grasped here on earth? This makes for excitement and diminishes the chances of any boredom taking over. Take a moment with each other and renew your commitment to keep growing together.

- *What potential for more happiness in your relationship do you see right now?*
- *What steps are you ready to take to develop that potential?*

Growth takes place one day at a time.

Providing A Meaningful Presence

Recently, a bright attorney returned with her husband from a conference for married couples. She remarked how the speakers were interesting and provided much food for thought. She added, "But for the most part, there was no heart." She revealed how she became aware of St. Paul's expression, "Sounding brass and tinkling cymbal."

We can immerse ourselves so in work, projects and causes that we really have little to say to each other, our children and our friends. If love is the measure, maybe we can try to add a "touch of love" to each phone call, letter, meeting and encounter with those we love and work with today. It isn't only quantity but the quality of our presence to those around us that gives true meaning to our presence with others.

> • *What do you bring to others with your presence?*
> • *What are you bringing to each other today*
> *with your presence?*

Growth takes place one day at a time.

The Calling Within

I once watched a little boy work his way through a crowd and perch himself atop a fence to catch a view of a parade. He seemed steadfast in his determination to get a good look. I think we may need to exert a determined effort to get a good look at what is going on inside ourselves.

How do we feel the gentle nudge, the stirring restlessness, the discomforting challenge, or a soothing calm that whispers to us? We need to provide for some quiet amidst our hectic and demanding day. Can we hear the stirring over the busy sounds and voices of the day? It takes a special effort to take a few minutes of our day and tune into the inner life that is calling for our attention.

- *Share your views about your efforts to develop more awareness of the hidden life within you.*
- *Talk to each other about what a spiritual life means to you.*

Growth takes place one day at a time.

Contacting The Obvious

We are becoming more conscious of our environment. There are calls for action that would help preserve the natural settings around us, and help establish a safer balance in the use of our natural resources. All this begins with an awareness of what is. Everything leaps out at us once we make an effort to notice.

Do we see the same things day after day? Do we drive the same route each day? Are we a victim of habit only? Look around for what is and see if we can slow down our gaze to take in what we see. Let what we see show us its uniqueness, its specialness, its liveliness and beauty. Slow down to really see.

Begin with really seeing your partner, your children and others. Observe the inanimate as well as the animate around you. Appreciate your awareness today.

• How confined are you to the routines in your life?
• Take a moment today to really notice your partner. Be willing to share what you notice.

Growth takes place one day at a time.

Closing The Gaps

We are beginning to realize how small our world really is. Television, science and technology of all kinds enable us to draw back our fences and close down some of the barriers that have kept whole nations of people closed off and alone.

In our marriages, there are barriers, sometimes subtle, that keep us apart from each other. When we identify these barriers and claim our responsibility for maintaining their existence, we are in a better position to do something about them. Are there any barriers in the form of noticeable obstacles that continue to surface in your relationship? What are the noticeable patterns that you can identify?

• Spend some time with each other, and check out what obstacles or barriers you are aware of in your relationship that may be keeping you distant from each other.
• Share with each other your feelings when you feel alone and isolated.

Growth takes place one day at a time.

Actions Reflecting Our Words

It is decorative to place a plaque on the wall stating that our house is a home filled with peace and open to all who come. It is good to renew those sentiments and good intentions by evaluating the atmosphere that is usually present. Are our hearts and minds really open to all who live there? It is so easy to forget our good intentions and so easy to set aside our aims.

Does our home truly reflect our beliefs about loving each other, encouraging each other as family? Are we different toward each other when guests, friends or relatives are present? Consider the way we treat each other and the atmosphere we are trying to have in our home.

• *Reflect on your home, and note if what is going on reflects your good intentions and the symbols that express those good intentions.*

Growth takes place one day at a time.

Faith-Filled Relationship

A newspaper writer once described faithfulness as not having an affair, not leaving, nor cheating on our partner. That description lacks the positive thrust of a faith-filled relationship.

To be faithful is to have the faith that the person we are married to is full of mystery that is open daily for discovery. A daily renewal of this faith can relieve us of the temptation of sure mindedness toward our partner, which can make our life together contain so much "sameness" and make it a "ho hum" experience. Renew your faithfulness today by setting aside some time for appreciating and thanking your partner for being a gift to you.

• How do you translate faithfulness?
• How is your faithfulness expressed and lived out
in your relationship?

Growth takes place one day at a time.

Continuing Our Discovery

In a throw away society, some couples consider throwing away their marriage. One of the reasons given is that "we have lost the spark and we can't find it." They are usually referring to the initial attraction of those early years, the infatuation, the chemistry, the excitement. All involve the thrill of discovery.

Ideally this discovery should continue on even though the thrill of that early discovery is no longer present. Years pass and new discoveries continue. We can savor each new phase we experience with each other. This may be the newness of parenthood, of each new child, of changing careers, of a new house. Each bend in the road of our journey together is new and capable of providing opportunity for mutual creation and enthusiasm. Seize each precious opportunity and you will not have to mourn the loss of the old spark.

- *What new discoveries have you been experiencing
in your relationship?*
- *How important is it to nourish and nurture such an approach
in your relationship?*

Growth takes place one day at a time.

Discovering Our Poverty

Poverty is often linked with an absence of material goods or money. It can also be linked with deficiency and the absence of those gifts and qualities we wish we possessed such as intelligence, good health, talents, and so on. When we recognize and admit these absences, we also experience true poverty. These recognitions are not easily followed by acceptance. We often try to offer excuses and attempt to cover them up somehow.

Facing our own poverty is difficult but it can be a important step in our attempts at personal growth. Accepting what is does not mean complacency or unwillingness to change. It is the first step in becoming honest with ourselves and thus, more open to the true gifts we do have.

• *Spend a little quiet time yourself and then share with your partner your awareness of your poverty.*

Growth takes place one day at a time.

Sing Our Song

"Sing a new song." It is not easy to sing or hum a tune when we feel down. Music and song, however, express a variety of moods. When we tune into what is around us, it can become easy to be discouraged and depressed. We hear of war, of insurrection, of life being snuffed out senselessly. There is great unrest in our society. In our own personal lives we see illness, death of those close to us, family turmoil, unemployment, married friends splitting up, and perhaps, we ourselves are weighed down with some things that are difficult to expose.

We may want to cry out. Who can sing? What is there to sing about? We need to recognize our own mood, our own sense of futility, of frustration and even despair. Can we share our thoughts and feelings without being termed a complainer? If so, we are fortunate and blessed. Thank your partner for being there for you and ask that he or she continue to be there for you.

- *Does your life allow for you to feel good about your world and the people in it?*
- *What is your new song today? Why not sing it together?*

Growth takes place one day at a time.

Taking It All In

We all have experiences that remind us of how really fortunate we are. The marvelous sights of nature, the sounds of music, the birth of a child, the gentle touch of our partner, the many things that stir our hearts. There are little twists and turns in our life, distractions, a business, our daily routine, that can block our senses from taking in many of these situations. We need to make time for minute vacations, stops along the way to rest our minds and bodies.

Do you know how to relax? Can you slow yourself down and simply let yourself be? Take time to center yourself. This is difficult for some of us, especially if we are constantly on the go.

- *Slow yourself down and slowly look around.*
- *Try to appreciate what you see and hear.*

Growth takes place one day at a time.

Our Signals Within

A feeling of emptiness can enter into our lives at strange and unexpected times. It may cause us to wonder if we are doing the right thing, in the right place and would be better off someplace else, with someone else. A certain restlessness strikes within all of us.

It need not move us into alarm or hasty changes we could later regret. It can be a positive sign and a call for an assessment of what may be going on in our lives. It can be difficult to place our finger exactly on this trouble spot. With calm persistence and effort to listen carefully to our thought associations and their accompanying feelings, we can often come up with something helpful.

- *Allow yourself to consider how you become aware of the internal signals inside of you calling for some attention from you.*
- *Can you share these awarenesses with your partner, or must you keep them to yourself?*

Growth takes place one day at a time.

Right? At What Cost?

As a couple, do we find ourselves arguing a lot? Does the bottom line come down to who is right and who is wrong? Sometimes this is caused by a subtle belief operating that all has to be separated into neat categories of black and white. It is like we can hear, "is so-is not-did so-did not."

Hanging on to such absolutes and reflecting no compromise or room for uncertainty make for a lot of arguments and frustration. Often such rigid posture goes unchanged, and we remain entrenched in our position of "all or nothing." Examine the positions you take when you and your partner argue, and note how you might feel when your position or conclusions are challenged.

> • *Do you take everything personally?*
> • *Must you conquer and win at all costs?*

Growth takes place one day at a time.

Reflection

Reflection invites us to tune in with our minds and hearts to the meaning and value of certain persons, places and things. In short, we begin to learn how to pay attention. We become conscious of their importance to us and what place we want them to have in our lives. We come to appreciate the silence of the moment and how we feel being present with ourselves.

We may struggle with setting aside the time, the place to begin. With practice and a calm resolution, we can attempt to give reflection a definite place in our day. Be steady in your resolve each day. Be consistent and continue to seek within yourself and each other through sharing.

> • *Are you maintaining a steady intention to set aside time each day for reflection?*
> • *Are you able to interest your partner in your sharing moments?*
> • *How could reflection help you in your personal life?*
> • *What effect could this have on your relationship?*

Growth takes place one day at a time.

Adding Skills to Our Intentions

Most of us strive to be happy and successful, especially in our marriage. We also realize how difficult this is. The divorce statistics strongly suggest that even with the best of intentions many relationships fail. All of us need to add certain skills to our good intentions. Skills such as becoming good communicators, good listeners, effective negotiators and problem solvers, sensitive and caring lovers, to name a few. These attributes for our relationship are learned skills and it takes persistent effort, goodwill and mutual help from each other in order to succeed.

Are you in agreement on the importance of gaining these skills in order to strengthen your relationship and give to each other the happiness and success that you as a couple rightly deserve? Consider where you are as a couple regarding the skills just mentioned and discuss your thoughts and feelings about them. What steps can you as a couple take in order to improve these skills in your marriage?

- *What skills would you like to learn or improve on?*
- *How could such effort benefit you and your relationship?*

Growth takes place one day at a time.

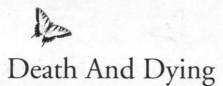

Death And Dying

We hear of death all around us. We watch it on the news, observe it occurring on the screen and maybe, we experienced it taking a family member or relative. We may feel a sense of numbness or even callousness to the death process.

On a personal level, there is a dying process that often escapes our attention. We can have a personal mourning for our youth, opportunity wasted, friendships that never survived, a lost vibrancy and intimacy in our marriage. We recognize many opportunities that "coulda, shoulda" been, but never were. Nevertheless, we can commit ourselves again today to keeping on, to learning from these flash memories and continue our belief that our lives are not without purpose and our days are committed to doing the best we can. Some time spent sharing our thoughts and feelings could be helpful.

- *What personal losses have you experienced in your life?*
- *What helps you deal with death, dying, and the other personal losses in your life?*

Growth takes place one day at a time.

Trust Brings Comfort

Many of us experience a lack of trust in our world. We don't trust politicians, unions, bosses, employees, even religion sometimes becomes victim to our mistrust. Trust is different from confidence. Trust is less dependent on evidence and is more an intuitive process.

It is derived from the German word *Trost*, meaning comfort. It contains an unquestionable belief in someone and a reliance on that person. It is not dependent on strategies. It is freely given. It can easily be seen in the eyes of a little child who appears open and willing to risk. When we trust ourselves, we enter into the process of discovering and creating who we are. When we trust another, we are able to let that person into our life. Fear stops the flow of trust and we direct our energy to protecting ourselves from anticipated dangers. Our relationships with others suffer. Trust enriches our experiences; fear robs it. Trust brings comfort and peace.

- *What are some of the ways you experience trust in your relationship?*
- *How is your trust challenged or hindered in your relationship?*
- *What could you personally do to build greater trust in your relationship?*

Growth takes place one day at a time.

Remarks That Sting

Where is the justice? We hear of others shouting how unfair the world is and how unrelenting and cruel people can be. We sometimes feel the sting that springs from insensitivity, uncaring and cruelty from another. It hurts the most when it comes from those we are close to.

Do we ever feel an antagonism or hurt from remarks made to us by people close to us? Do we feel like we want to attack or withdraw when this happens? Do we feel victimized and wonder why it continues to occur even when we have made known the pain it causes us?

- *Consider your own efforts to deal with the remarks, the comments, the words that often wound you.*
- *Consider the ways you deal with this in your life and how it may be affecting your marriage relationship.*
- *What can you do to avoid causing others to feel the sting of your words?*

Growth takes place one day at a time.

December 6

Hope In Our Life

Hope has sometimes been referred to as the "forgotten virtue." Perhaps that is because it is often couched between two close friends, Faith and Love. It is said that there is no real psychology of hope and that it is frequently passed off as a simple wish. At Christmas time, hope seems to get a boost. There is a spirit of acceptance, and a hopeful attitude for the holiday.

What does hope bring to you for your life? Is this a once a year experience and feeling for you? In every therapist's office, there are hundreds of stories with different variations and substance. As a therapist, I am in close contact with the workings of hope. I think it is of sufficient importance to consider hope and its meaning for us. It will be the theme for the next few reflections. In the meantime, consider what hope means to you and share with your partner.

- *Can you recognize any need for hope in your life?*
- *What is it that you hope for?*

Growth takes place one day at a time.

Hope Is Realistic

The implication that is present when we say we have hope is that we are in some kind of trouble. It is often seen as the opposite of despair. But that would limit our interpretation. Hope is positive and realistic. It has its roots in realism. It isn't some sort of vague yearning after something unattainable.

We do have to be careful, however, lest we relate it to some kind of magical wishing, a kind of wishing, for something to happen and removing ourselves from doing something about it ourselves. I think of the words, "pray as if it all depended upon God, and act as if it all depended upon us." We are taking responsibility for our part in the equation and not asking God alone to do the job

• How realistic is your hope?
• Consider its implication for yourself and your partner.

Growth takes place one day at a time.

Hope Is Clear And Directed

Essential ingredients of our hope are that it be clear and directed. Hope in "something" or "for something to happen" leaves us non-directed and vague in our thoughts and direction. This leaves room for magical thinking and possible illusion. It is important to let another know what we hope for. This can involve risk, but it does help prevent us from setting ourselves up for the negative questions, "But what if..." or "why bother, it won't happen anyway." It is like telling ourselves not to hope for anything, then we won't be disappointed.

Are we directing our hope clearly? Are there built in "what if's" or any other limitations or qualifications that we attach to our hopes? This can be a good opportunity for self-evaluation and an opportunity to discuss and share with our partner.

> • *How could hope be your gift to each other?*
> • *How clear and directed is your hope?*

Growth takes place one day at a time.

Imagination Assisting Our Hope

Do we allow ourselves to hope, or are we afraid that by hoping, we show our hand and reveal ourselves more than we are prepared for? Allowing ourselves to acknowledge our hopes to ourselves can mean that we are finally opening ourselves to our honest longings and desires. This process takes the gift of imagination, which is a powerful ingredient, and drives our hopes. It is an important ally. It is enemy to the types of thinking that place everything into mental boxes containing all absolutes and leaving no room for possibilities and facts that are simply not in yet.

Do we try to make a sure thing out of everything or anyone in our life? Opening ourselves to the power of our imagination can free us to walk around more freely amidst the thoughts, fantasies and feelings within.

• Share your thoughts and experiences regarding your hopes, and how you might better employ your imagination to work for you.

Growth takes place one day at a time.

Balancing Our Hopes

There are times when we recognize that our hopes do not erase all those areas of hopelessness we feel at times. We can, however, learn to mark those areas by acknowledging them to ourselves first and then attempt to face them directly. We do this not by despairing ourselves, but by seeking consciously to have a positive intention not to allow hopelessness to pollute the areas of possibilities in our life.

We need to keep a balanced view of the things we can do and the things we can't do. The prayer of the person struggling to hold his or her addiction at bay is appropriate here–"God grant me the serenity to accept the things I cannot change, the courage to change the things I can, and the wisdom to know the difference." (Serenity Prayer). To keep the three in balance and in place is to stay free from intolerable burdens.

* *How do your hopes encourage and lift you up?*
* *How can you nurture your hopes and the hopes of your partner?*

Growth takes place one day at a time.

Hope And Hopelessness

In the earliest stages, hope contains our own beliefs and convictions that there is a way out of our difficulty. Things can work out. We can handle and manage the problem or situation. There are solutions. We have a sense of the possible. It may be difficult, but I can have it and it is possible. This is wishful thinking in the good sense of the term. It is also spirited in the sense that we can relate our hopes to the longer term consequences. We can look up to those hopes, those deeper aspirations and desires that often escape us as we live our busy lives. A sense of hopelessness occurs when we see no possibilities, no way out, no exit.

In our lives, we can expect at some time to experience both a sense of hope and a sense of hopelessness. Can we appreciate and respect the humanness of our hopes as well as our sense of hopelessness? Can we share these experiences, thoughts and feelings with someone, especially our partner?

- *When do you feel the most hopeful?*
- *When do you feel hopeless?*

Growth takes place one day at a time.

Our Inside Protections

We are surrounded by many sounds. To some extent, we get used to them. They serve as a backdrop for our work, our activities, our conversations.

There also are those things that keep us at a distance from others and they are inside of us. These are the protections that we wrap around ourselves to avoid being hurt or pained. They are meant to provide us with the security we feel we need. This same process, however, can leave us feeling lonely and alone. It becomes a risk for us to reach out and trust. It means taking a chance, opening ourselves to possible misunderstandings by others and even unintentional harmful remarks.

- *What are your protections and how do you experience them operating in your relationship with your partner?*

Growth takes place one day at a time.

Words Of Power

Words have great power. They can support and encourage, and they can hurt and discourage. Sometimes just the right word is all it takes to lift someone's spirit and help another to face a day with new courage.

Our words are like husks. They cover what is inside. It is not the husk that carries our meaning, it is the seed inside. It is ourselves. We provide the meaning. We all learn at an early age to use words. We do not easily learn to share the kernel of ourselves with others. This takes trust, honesty and a willingness to become our true selves with others. This is not easy and we need support, insight and the courage to learn about ourselves. It is important to become aware of just what our words are saying and bringing to others.

- *Spend a little time in the next few reflections considering your words with the people you live and work with, especially your partner.*
- *Do you feel safe to express your thoughts and feelings?*
- *What are you doing to create an atmosphere of acceptance and respect for each other's opinion?*

Growth takes place one day at a time.

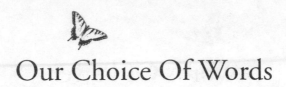

Our Choice Of Words

Our words accompany a certain style of communicating. It depends on our intentions. If we intend to simply maintain peace and tranquility and not cause any waves or any perceived distress, we usually choose words that are on the light side. We talk about the weather, sports, television and those things that are really outside of ourselves and devoid of any serious emotion. What we say does not get us emotionally involved with the other person. There is a place for this kind of bantering and light usage of words. It can be helpful if we know this to be our intention.

Our words can take on a more serious void when the other person in our life is starving for the grain inside the husk. If we are unwilling to share that grain for some reason, we are withholding ourselves and encouraging a starvation diet.

- *Consider this style and the intention behind your words, and share with your partner.*
- *Is this a major style in your relationship?*

Growth takes place one day at a time.

Style And Words

Protection of ourselves comes in many different forms. We raise our hands to ward off incoming blows. We instinctively pull back from something we perceive could physically harm us. We protect ourselves when we feel threatened emotionally and spiritually. This is very helpful for us and we need to appreciate the role of protection in our lives.

Our words must be considered in the light of our intentions. If we intend to control another and let them know that our way is the only way, or we intend to direct and tell others the way things should be, then we intend to convert others to our way of thinking and doing. This can work when we are selling a product, but it does not work well when we are trying to build a loving and caring relationship. This is not a bad style, but it is a style accompanied by some form of control. This can make for problems in our relationships, especially when one or both are attempting to treat each other equally and with openness.

- *Consider your relationship in the light of this style in your relationship with your partner.*
- *In what ways do you try to convince or influence your partner with what you say?*

Growth takes place one day at a time.

An Invitation To Explore Together

Sometimes we want to explore and discuss an issue without committing ourselves to any direction or conclusion. Here again, our aim and intention are vital. In this instance, we are trying to be open and honest in our efforts to discuss and explore. We have no investment in being right or making the other person wrong. Our words reflect an attitude of acceptance and the message conveyed to another is "we are equals," "let's explore together," "there is no question of who is right or wrong."

We are offering to each other our thoughts of possibilities such as, "could it be," "I wonder if," "is it possible that." There is a tentativeness about our position and we say so. This enables the other person to experience a searching and an honest curiosity about the topic or issue under consideration.

*• Discuss this particular approach and style of communicating,
and note how this may be reflected in your words
and in your relationship.*

Growth takes place one day at a time.

Sharing From Our Heart

There are times when we need, and even want, to go beyond chitchatting and making light conversation. There are times when we want to share ourselves more deeply. We want to make known our true feelings and thoughts. We trust enough to do this and we have reached the stage in our relationship when we can risk telling our partner what ordinarily we may keep to ourselves.

Our intention is to share intimately our deepest feelings. We attempt to share what we are aware of deeply within ourselves. Our awareness extends to what we are most in touch with inside of ourselves. All is at our disposal and we feel free to express ourselves openly and honestly. Often, this is ideal and good for the most significant relationships in our lives.

• Can you share your deepest feelings with each other?
If so, how? If not, why not?
• What could you do to help develop this style of
communication with each other?

Growth takes place one day at a time.

Faithful To Our Beliefs

In my reading, I was led to the first chapter of Luke in the New Testament and the story of Zachariah, the father of John the Baptist. Someone referred to Zachariah as the patron saint of dry spells. He and his wife, Elizabeth, prayed for many years to have a child of their own. He was very faithful to his duties in the temple and to his prayer, but he no longer believed. When the Angel Gabriel informed him that his wife was to have a child, he simply didn't believe it. "It's not possible–look how old she is, for God's sake–do you expect me to believe...?"

How natural a response. He continued his plea to God each day, but his heart wasn't really in it. What of our faithfulness to our beliefs? Are we really open to what our hopes and prayers could bring us? Do we really believe that new life is possible as we grow old, together?

> • *How are your beliefs affecting the way you live*
> *your lives together?*
> • *What do you see are your strongest beliefs?*
> *Does your partner share these with you?*

Growth takes place one day at a time.

Never Losing Our Creativity

An important choice we all have as couples is to choose to live our lives enmeshed with daily activities and busy things alone or make room for those things that challenge us to grow. We are called to maintain our aliveness as individuals and as couples.

The greatest gift we can give to our partner is to remain vibrant and alive ourselves. We come to know each other and ourselves by continuing to create—and make new what is not yet there in our marriage.

The fortunate among us can understand what it means to procreate. When we no longer can do so, our ability to create does not stop. We must then find ways to direct our creative energies within ourselves and with each other.

The suffering, the difficult times, the hardships and disappointments can bind us closely together. It is also our ability to help each other grow and foster our creative energy with each other that will tie us into married oneness.

- *How are you attempting to use your creative talent?*
- *How can you invite each other to continue growing in your relationship?*

Growth takes place one day at a time.

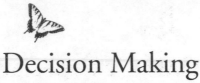

Decision Making

Sometimes we are faced with having to make certain decisions. We have done our best to gather the necessary facts and evaluate the circumstances involved. It takes a certain wisdom to know when we need more information and when we simply need to make a decision.

We can pray for the gift of discernment. This spiritual gift still leaves us with the task of doing our homework. We need to make certain that we are open to the inner stirrings and the movement of the spirit within us. We need to recognize the pulls and tugs that call for recognition and respectful attention. As we seek to make those necessary decisions that affect our lives and those we love, we attempt to bring into awareness as much of ourselves as we are able.

- *What goes into your decision making process?*
- *How do you feel about your ability to make decisions individually and with your partner?*
- *What issues are currently calling for your decision?*

Growth takes place one day at a time.

A Time Of Expectation

Today is designated the shortest day of the year and the beginning of winter in the northern hemisphere. It seems so clear and definite. The passage from one season to another. The end of fall and the beginning of winter. How far in advance are we looking? Can we imagine the activity of spring when we still see the snow on the ground?

In our daily lives, we do not experience these transitions clearly nor easily. The changes we experience come slowly and often painfully. Change is the only constant in our lives. We are either moving forward or going backwards. There really is no standing still.

Many of us are experiencing the excitement of the holiday. Our hopes are heightened. Our spirits are invigorated and we may experience the excitement involved in anticipation. What are you anticipating? Is this a sign of a personal renewal of faith and hope for you?

- *Discuss and share your anticipation, your hopes and vision for yourself and each other.*

Growth takes place one day at a time.

Delightful Surprises

Surprises contain hidden invitations, unplanned for reactions and responses. Our lives can become grooved and filled with sameness and predictability. We can lose the ability to celebrate surprises in our life and fail to allow for unplanned events and occurrences.

Does our life become so planned, so controlled that we no longer experience any surprises? Do we offer surprises to each other? When do we offer to each other some little gift of surprise—an unexpected phone call, a flower for no reason, maybe just an unexpected love note? Give to each other the gift of being able to make delightful discoveries through pure surprises. This is serendipity.

- *How do you and your partner celebrate surprises in your relationship and avoid sameness and boredom?*
- *How can serendipity help your relationship grow in aliveness?*

Growth takes place one day at a time.

Acknowledge Creativity

Just two more days to Christmas and there is mention of a new gadget, a new toy, a new piece of equipment, just as we thought we had seen and heard it all. It can be so tiring, so frantic, and perhaps, we may have even a kind thought for Scrooge and bah-humbug, as if to admit we can identify with the old geezer.

But on further thought, our reflection today could contain some praise and admiration for men like Bardeen, Brattan and Shockley, who on this day in 1947 experienced final success and brought into being the first transistor. This made possible the many electronic miracles to follow.

Take a silent moment of thanks for all those who make and create. Consider your own efforts today. Especially those you have made and are making for this holiday to be just a bit more special.

- *See the labor and appreciate the laborer today.*
- *Look for a way to express your appreciation and respect.*

Growth takes place one day at a time.

Let Our Light Shine

There is a busyness all around us today. People are moving at a rapid pace. Some are buying, and some are just looking. Music fills the airwaves as we listen for our favorite carol or seasonal song.

The threats of world unrest and the absence of peace cause us to pause for some serious reflection on the meaning of it all. Many today are living in darkness—a darkness and despair associated with those addicted to some kind of drug, the poor who live with hopelessness, the victims of violence and abuse, the chronically ill, and so on. How does the light shine when there is so much darkness?

We are reminded that our own comfort can perhaps caution us and make us pause to reflect on how we can bring a little light to the world around us. Our world, our own limited world, reflects some of that darkness. How can we bring that little light of ours to shine? Let it shine! Let it shine! Let it shine!

- *How are you hiding your light under a basket?*
- *How can you be a light for each other and others around you?*

Growth takes place one day at a time.

Learning The True Meaning

For many, this is a very special day. There are many gifts to open and share and a gathering together of relatives and friends. This may be a day for a special visit or perhaps a day of sadness, loneliness and isolation.

However, somewhere in all of this there is a seed of hope and a deeper awareness that the birthday celebrated carries a deep spiritual meaning. We are reminded of the paradox of this day. It conveys thoughts of grandeur, and yet simplicity. Scholars tell us that the birthplace of Jesus was really quite crude and dirty. Perhaps we should not let our imagination about the stable paint too pretty a picture and instead allow for the reality that it was truly as dingy a place as we could ever imagine.

This suggests to us that if such a place could be visited by the Holy One, then maybe, we can all rejoice that this same Holy One can be born in us also. We are very much like the stable, with our own crudeness, our sinfulness and our spiritual blindness. We rejoice today because no one is excluded.

• How is this day special for you?
• How do you bring yourself as a gift to each other?

Growth takes place one day at a time.

How Can This Be?

There are circumstances and events occurring in our lives to which we can only say, "How can this be?" We haven't prepared for it, we haven't asked for it, it is simply here and we attempt to acknowledge its meaning for us. We really don't know why certain things happen, and we are left with a simple response, "How can this be?"

Are there such events and circumstances occurring in our life, and how are we responding? Does it even matter one way or the other to us? Are we simply willing to just let it be? Maybe we want to "fit" the event or circumstance into our life by saying "yes" to it and allow ourselves to learn something from it. Do we ever give it a spiritual meaning?

Allow yourself to consider the question. "How can this be" and the circumstances when you utter these same words in your life and in your relationship.

• Are there events or circumstances in your life
you have difficulty accepting?
• What response would best allow you to move on with your life
and grow from your experience?
• How can you help each other deal constructively with the
unplanned events in your lives?

Growth takes place one day at a time.

Joy In Our Life

How much in our lives are we doing for the sheer joy of it? How much laughter is there? Our answer to these two questions, if answered honestly, may surprise us. Though we can allow ourselves to admit that both are important, we may seldom consider just where these two are for us.

We may tend to be skeptical and mistrustful of them because of our suspicion that they reflect either insecurity or a lack of seriousness on our part. Is our vision of our world one of a problem to be solved rather than a joy to be lived? We could be fostering a depressive kind of seriousness that weighs heavily on the spirit. How are you opening yourself up to the joy and laughter in your life? Victor Borgia once said, "Laughter measures the distance between two people."

- *What gives you joy and makes you laugh?*
- *How do you give joy to each other in your marriage?*

Growth takes place one day at a time.

Turning Up Those Inspirations

Inspirations for our lives come from a variety of sources, both outside and inside of ourselves. We need to be listening for both. Our dreams can reflect inner strife and struggle but they can also reflect and inspire us to consider new areas of growth in our lives.

Our thoughts flow in and out daily. Often, our thoughts are lost or simply placed aside and given no particular attention. These same thoughts could be repeating themselves and signaling to us invitations and inspiration for our personal growth and happiness. We need to learn to pay attention to these inner movements within ourselves lest we ourselves become destroyers of our own dreams and inspiration. Let's listen to our dreams, our thoughts, and become more aware of what we think about during our day.

- *What inspirations for your life, for your marriage, are you hearing today?*
- *How are you nurturing and supporting each other's dreams and inspirations?*

Growth takes place one day at a time.

Light Bearers

The many lights we see at the holidays reflect a festive atmosphere. Light has been a symbol and a reference point for poets, scholars and preachers for many years. Milton referred to light as the offspring of heaven. It was the first to occur in the work of creation. Light has been referred to as the symbol of truth and we may have looked for it in the eyes of another. Jesus refers to himself as the light and we are asked to walk wisely in the light.

What is the light that we seek? Is it spiritual awareness, truth in each other, sincerity and respect, deep faith and goodness? It can be all of the above and more. Who is light for us? Who brings joy, forgiveness, support, encouragement to us? Who are the light bearers in our life—those with whom we live, share and work?

- *Consider how you can be light bearers to each other in your marriage and family.*
- *What in your life is seeking recognition and understanding?*

Growth takes place one day at a time.

Persevere In The Light

We are facing some massive problems in our world. As the year winds down, we hear references to these problems and we can easily ask the question, is there no light at the end of the tunnel? Dare we believe that out of all this darkness we can still see some light? Is our belief so shaken that we give up hoping, give up believing that life is stronger than death, that hope is stronger than despair and that goodness and truth will prevail?

The motto for the Christopher's is, "It is better to light one candle than curse the darkness." Our candle may seem so insignificant when we consider the mess we see our world in. When we add our little light to the millions of other lights, we form a bond of strength. These are the little acts of service, of caring, of giving and forgiving. Yes, we are the light of the world.

• *Share your thoughts and feelings with your partner, especially the effort it will take to persevere in your light.*
• *Have you ever considered yourself to be a light for others? If so, how? If not, why not?*

Growth takes place one day at a time.

Family Memories

We all have our view of what makes a healthy and happy family. We may not agree on all the ingredients making up such a family. We all have tried to live with our realities as we experience them. This, obviously, includes some myths here and there.

As we look back at our own families, we realize that the word "dysfunctional" can probably apply to all of us in some form or other. We don't have to come from families pained by alcohol or violence to be scarred. What memories do we have of our years growing up? What myths are we carrying around with us pertaining to our own family?

What has been going on in our immediate family this past year in terms of taking care of each other's needs with patience and kindness? Share your thoughts and feelings with your partner–a good way to close out the old year and begin a new one.

- *What family traits did you bring to your marriage?*
- *What does family mean to you? Does your partner share your views? If so, how? If not, why not?*

Growth takes place one day at a time.

— *notes* —

notes